OVERLAND
through
Southern Africa

OVERLAND
through
Southern Africa

Willie & Sandra Olivier

Struik Publishers (Pty) Ltd
(a member of The Struik Publishing Group (Pty) Ltd)
Cornelis Struik House, 80 McKenzie Street
Cape Town 8001

Reg. No.: 54/00965/07

First published 1998

Managing editor: Annlerie van Rooyen
Editor: Thea Coetzee
Design manager: Janice Evans
Designer: Laurence Lemmon-Warde
Design assistant: Lellyn Creamer
Picture researcher: Carmen Swanepoel
Cartographer: Desireé Oosterberg
Indexer and proofreader: Lesley Hay-Whitton

Reproduction: Hirt & Carter Cape (Pty) Ltd
Printing and binding: Kyodo Printing Co (S'pore) Pte Ltd

The information in this book was correct at the time of going to press. While every effort has been made to ensure accuracy, some of the information will become outdated during the edition's life-span. The Publishers would appreciate advice relevant to this book for incorporation into subsequent editions. Please write to: The Editor, *Overland through Southern Africa*, Struik Publishers, P O Box 1144, Cape Town, 8000.

ISBN 1 86872 105 1

Front cover: *Vehicles snaking across a plain in the Richtersveld, South Africa's only mountain desert.*
Spine: *Steep or rocky descents must be negotiated in four-wheel drive low range.*
Back cover: *The Sani Pass winds to the summit of the Drakensberg in a series of tight U-bends and zigzags.*
Half title page: *One of the major attractions of the Richtersveld National Park is its rugged mountain scenery and isolation.*
Title page: *At sunset the Orange River and the mountains of the Richtersveld are transformed into a kaleidoscope of gold and soft pastel colours.*
Following pages: *A road vanishes into the snowy hills of the northeastern Free State nears Clarens.*

ACKNOWLEDGEMENTS
To all who joined us on various occasions and trips into the wilds of Southern Africa, we say thank you for your good company. A special word of thanks goes to our long-suffering editor, Thea Coetzee, who checked meticulously and always gave us a sympathetic ear. Our appreciation also goes to Annlerie van Rooyen for her understanding when we needed more time, and to all the Struik staff who contributed to this book.
WILLIE AND SANDRA OLIVIER, WINDHOEK, NAMIBIA

PICTURE CREDITS
SIL = Struik Image Library; PA = Photo Access
Shaen Adey (SIL): pp. 34, 35 (bottom), 51 (top left), 53 (top), 62, 74 (bottom). **Daryl Balfour:** pp. 22, 25, 90, 91, 92, 93 (top, bottom), 94 (top, bottom), 96–97, 98, 100 (top, bottom), 102, 103 (top, bottom), 104 (bottom), 105, 106–107, 166, 168–169. **Keith Begg (SIL):** pp. 115, 116, 120, 122 (top), 123 (top, bottom), 173. **Colour Library (SIL):** p. 80. **Roger de la Harpe:** [all SIL except p. 108]: pp. 65, 68, 72, 111 (top, bottom), 114, 117, 118–119, 124 (top), 125, 126, 127, 128–129. **Nigel Dennis (SIL):** pp. 9, 17, 44 (bottom), 45, 74 (top), 75, 78, 81, 82, 83 (bottom), 84, 85 (top), 86–87. **Gerhard Dreyer (SIL):** pp. 43 (bottom), 44 (top). **Jéan du Plessis:** Front cover, half-title page, title page, pp. 8, 12, 14, 147, 152, 153, 155, 157 (top, bottom), 158–159, 163, 171. **Nancy Gardiner:** Back cover, p. 58. **Leonard Hoffmann (SIL):** pp. 70, 71. **Jeremy Jowell:** p. 136 (bottom). **Walter Knirr:** [all SIL except pp. 63 (top), 83 (top), 154, 156]: pp. 19, 28, 41, 51 (top right), 54, 64. **Willie & Sandra Olivier:** Spine, pp. 11, 16, 101, 140, 143 (top), 144, 146 (top, bottom), 148–149. **Peter Pickford (SIL):** pp. 73, 142. **Peter Ribton (SIL):** p. 122 (bottom). **D. Rogers (PA – Getaway):** p. 113. **Mark Skinner (SIL):** p. 110. **D. Steele (PA – Getaway):** pp. 130, 132, 133, 135, 136 (top), 137, 162. **D. Steele (PA):** p. 165. **Hein von Hörsten:** [all SIL except pp. 6–7]: pp. 13, 30, 33, 35 (top), 38, 42, 43 (top), 46–47, 48, 50, 53 (bottom left, bottom right), 55 (top, bottom), 63 (bottom), 66–67, 145. **Lanz von Hörsten (SIL):** pp. 21, 31, 32, 36–37, 40, 61. **P. Wagner (PA – Getaway):** pp. 76–77, 134, 138–139, 143 (bottom), 164, 167. **Chanan Weiss:** pp. 56–57, 88, 95, 104 (top), 150, 160. **Keith Young (SIL):** p. 60.

Contents

Introduction

Southern Africa is a region of scenic contrasts – parched deserts, towering mountains, sun-drenched beaches and virgin forests. Here, too, can be found the Namib, one of the oldest deserts in the world, as well as the pristine waterways of the Okavango Delta and the world's smallest, richest floral kingdom. Adding to the ever-changing landscapes are the bare dunes and vast plains of the Kalahari, woodlands, waterfalls and grasslands.

Equally spectacular is the sub-continent's wildlife heritage. The endless plains and woodlands of many game sanctuaries are home to the Big Five (elephant, rhino, lion, leopard and buffalo) as well as giraffe, zebra and a variety of antelope. Following in the wake of herds of antelope are the entire spectrum of predators: lion, leopard, cheetah, wild dog, hyena and many more. Birdlife is prolific and, with well over 1 000 bird species recorded on the sub-continent, birding is a popular pastime.

Southern Africa also has an incredibly rich variety of plants and one of the most amazing floral spectacles in the world – Namaqualand's seasonal display of flowers. Among its wealth of plants are the 'halfmens' *(Pachypodium namaquanum)*, the bizarre-looking welwitschia, baobabs, palm trees, mopane woodlands and a diversity of succulents.

Another attraction of the sub-continent is its people and the rich diversity of its cultures. Here you will find the last of the hunter-gatherer San and also the pastoral Himba – people little altered by changes brought about by 'civilization'. Several archaeological sites provide an insight into the region's earlier inhabitants, among them Great Zimbabwe, the most significant site in sub-Saharan Africa, and Twyfelfontein, the site of Africa's largest concentrations of rock engravings and rock paintings.

However, the wild places of Southern Africa are rapidly disappearing because of the sub-continent's growing population and the advances of 'civilization'. Tracks of a decade ago are now high-quality gravel roads, and tar roads are fast replacing yesteryear's potholed roads. At the time of writing, two major road projects, the Trans-Caprivi and the Trans-Kalahari highways, were nearing completion. Several other major road projects have been announced, including a 156-km coastal road between the KwaZulu-Natal village of Hluhluwe and the Mozambican border and the Wild Coast road between Port Edward and Port St John's.

As little as a decade ago, getting to these wild and remote places was an expedition in itself, part of the fun, but things have changed and nowadays the bone-jarring journeys between places such as Nata and Maun in Botswana or from Rundu to Katima Mulilo in Namibia are something of the past. Despite these changes, however, there are still a number of relatively untravelled byways and back roads just waiting to be explored. There are still places where you can be lulled to sleep by the plaintive 'Good Lord, deliver us' call of the fierynecked nightjar and where you may be woken up by the harsh, crowing notes of the redbilled francolin, places where the seemingly endless

Opposite: *The rugged tracks of the Richtersveld are best negotiated in a sturdy four-wheel drive vehicle.*
Above: *A baobab etched against the sky, one of the symbols of wildest Africa.*

plains blend into the distant horizon and where the eerie call of the spotted hyena sends shivers down your spine.

Overland through Southern Africa is a book of ideas – ideas to stimulate your sense of adventure to discover these magical places. You will not find detailed route directions, nor GPS (Global Positioning System) co-ordinates to guide you.

While a sense of adventure is a prerequisite if you want to embark on a trip into the wilds, you will need more than an adventurous spirit. Exchanging the highways for the byways requires careful planning, knowledge of the terrain and the area into which you intend to venture, and common sense. Poor preparation, ignorance and carelessness can not only cause inconvenience, but can result in injury and even death.

As a result of the improvement in the standard of roads throughout the sub-continent, some of the routes described in this book can be done in two-wheel drive cars. Others are negotiable by sedan car, except for optional four-wheel drive sections, while yet other are strictly 4x4. The latter should not be tackled alone and parties should consist of at least two four-wheel drive vehicles. No matter how well prepared and cautious you are, things do go wrong in the bush and assistance could be hundreds of kilometres or days away. Once you venture away from the highways in Botswana, Namibia, Mozambique and Zambia, parties should consist of at least three four-wheel drive vehicles, equipped to deal with any emergency.

Virtually the whole of Southern Africa has summer rainfall. After heavy rains, back roads often become impassable, even to four-wheel drive vehicles, and floodplains, such as the Busanga Plain in Zambia's Kafue National Park, become inaccessible. In summer, temperatures in excess of 40 degrees Centigrade are not

9

uncommon in many parts of Southern Africa. In addition, game viewing is usually less rewarding as the animals disperse widely. As a general rule the months between April and September are, therefore, the best to explore Southern Africa's wild places. Not only are temperatures more bearable, but this is also the best time for game viewing. During these months the animals tend to congregate around the waterholes and along the rivers, and the vegetation cover is less dense, making game viewing considerably easier than just after the rains. Another advantage is that the risk of contracting malaria is reduced.

When travelling to any country in Southern Africa, bear in mind that you must have the necessary travel (passport, visa) and vehicle documentation (clearance and vehicle registration certificates). In South Africa, all this information is available free of charge to members of the Automobile Association. Alternatively, you should confirm your travel plans with the High Commission of the country concerned or, in the case of Mozambique, the Consulate-General.

Travelling to off-the-beaten-track destinations also requires taking all the necessary health precautions, a subject which is dealt with in more detail in the section Staying healthy in the bush (*see* page 20).

Finally, visiting the few remaining wild destinations in Southern Africa places a very special responsibility on you to protect them. With improved road access comes inevitable change and also increasing multitudes of tourists, until their numbers threaten the very existence of these places and the rationale of going there. Bear in mind that many of Southern Africa's ecosystems are extremely sensitive to any disturbance. Stick to existing tracks at all times – blazing your own trail is not only unattractive, but the damage caused to the environment can take decades to heal.

Respect other cultures and treat them with the same regard you expect from them. Wherever possible, ask for permission to use scarce resources such as water and firewood, or to camp in areas inhabited by local people. By obtaining information about their customs you will not only enrich yourself culturally, but will also help to undo the resentment that some indigenous people have against tourists.

Remember to take out whatever you take in. Do not bury any litter, as it is usually uncovered by animals or the elements. In addition to being unsightly, it can cause injury to animals and people, sometimes even resulting in the painful death of animals. Broken bottles can also shred tyres.

Another important point to remember is to respect the historical and archaeological heritage of Southern Africa. Under no circumstances should you touch, or spray water or any other substance onto, rock paintings or rock engravings. Also, do not be tempted to take away anything, for example petrified wood or archaeological artefacts, as a souvenir.

Right: *Plains littered with rocks and clumps of euphorbia bushes dominate the landscape around Palmwag in Damaraland.*

Choice of vehicle

Above: *The thick, loose sand of Bushmanland and Khaudum requires the tyres of the vehicle to be deflated and also means constant use of four-wheel drive.*

Although some of the routes described in this book are negotiable in a two-wheel drive vehicle, the advantages of exploring Southern Africa's off-the-beaten track destinations in a four-wheel drive vehicle cannot be over-emphasized. Most modern cars have an extremely low ground clearance and are not built to withstand the rigours of travelling for long distances on corrugated gravel roads. Also bear in mind that even gravel roads that are generally negotiable by sedan cars sometimes become badly corrugated during peak tourist seasons. After summer rains roads are often washed away and river crossings can be

tricky. Although the tarred roads in Zambia and Mozambique are being upgraded, some sections are still badly potholed, providing a test to the shock absorbers and suspension of even the most rugged four-wheel drive vehicles.

What is often the most important requirement to negotiate gravel tracks is high ground clearance. Much of Damaraland in Namibia, for example, is accessible in a two-wheel drive vehicle with high ground clearance. However, there will inevitably be a stretch of sand, a sandy river crossing or difficult departure angle that necessitates four-wheel drive.

Four-wheel drive vehicles are built to withstand the rigours of rocky terrain, deep sand, and wading through water and mud. In addition to better roadholding, a four-wheel drive vehicle instils in you the confidence that you will be able to get out of most tricky situations. Extended trips into the wilds require a vehicle that can take a heavy load and also has ample packing space – requirements that a sedan car generally cannot meet. Since you sit higher off the ground you have better vision, especially when viewing game.

In Southern Africa there is a wide range of four-wheel drive vehicles from which to choose. Your choice will ultimately be determined by your requirements – how far you intend travelling off the beaten track, the frequency of your journeys, the number of people that usually travel with you, as well as price and personal preference.

While the specifications of many of these vehicles are fairly similar, factors you should bear in mind are the torque and gear ratio, petrol versus diesel, tank capacity and estimated fuel range, load capacity and ground clearance. Other considerations include the approach, departure and roll-over angles, maximum wade depth and whether there is space for an additional battery and fuel tank. You should also pay attention to aspects such as the type of suspension, the track width, whether the vehicle is fitted with a differential lock, and whether it has all-time four-wheel drive, manual or automatic freewheeling hubs.

Another important aspect is vehicle accessories. One of the major considerations when planning a trip into the wilds is the availability of fuel. Some four-wheel drive vehicles have a maximum off-road fuel range of only 300 km, while many average about 500 km. On some trips, however, you will require fuel to cover 1 000 km or more to the next reliable refuelling stop, making it worthwhile to consider installing an additional fuel tank, rather than lugging around jerry cans.

Tyres are also a major consideration. While wide off-road tyres are very useful when travelling in sandy terrain, you should take extreme care when venturing into the rocky terrain of places such as Namibia's Kaokoveld with low-profile tyres, as they are easily shredded by the sharp stones.

Other accessories worth thinking about include a roof rack, bushbars, auxiliary driving lights, an additional battery, built-in

Above: A four-wheel drive vehicle is indispensable when launching boats along the coast. At the same time it places a responsibility on drivers not to disturb the sensitive ecology.

water tank and rooftop tent. Although not essential, a winch can be quite useful, especially when all other recovery techniques have been exhausted. However, it is one of the more expensive accessories and you should not be tempted to compromise quality for price. If you do invest in one, ensure that it is rated at least 1,5 times your vehicle's gross mass.

Having bought the means of transport to suit your needs does not necessarily mean that you are now ready to head off into the bush. Bush driving requires considerable skills and without these you might well get bogged down or suffer mechanical damage. First of all, you will have to familiarize yourself thoroughly with your vehicle. Often told is the sad story of the proud new owner of a four-wheel drive who found himself bogged down to the chassis on a sandy track far out in the bush. The harder he tried to extricate it, the deeper it sank into the sand. After several hours of sweating and at the point of despair, help finally arrived. 'Are the hubs locked?' the rescuer enquired. 'The what?' came the reply. On inspecting the front hubs, they were found to be in the free position. A flick of the hubs and a few shoves and the novice adventurer was on his way again.

To get to know your vehicle, the best advice is to start close to home with relatively easy obstacles and to progress gradually to more difficult and challenging terrain. The Hennops Off-road Trail is ideally situated for people in Gauteng wanting to familiarize themselves with their vehicles. The trail is designed for novice and experienced drivers. You can also get to know your vehicle and become more confident by joining organized

trail, such as the Kalahari 4x4 Trail (*see* page 80), conducted by Joppie Botes, or you could tackle some of the self-guided routes that are more and more often being opened on private property.

Off-road driving courses are becoming increasingly popular and are well worth considering. One-day courses are conducted by the Continental Off-road Academy at the Gerotek vehicle-testing facility near Hartbeespoort Dam. Some aspects covered in these courses include the dynamics of a four-wheel drive vehicle, as well as driving and winching techniques. Longer trips to Botswana and Lesotho are also offered. The instructors of the Academy have all taken part in and instructed on the Camel Trophy. Basic courses in 4x4 driving are also offered on a farm near Nelspruit by the Off-road Experience. The courses are conducted by the instructors and marshalls who have been involved in the Camel Adventure.

One of the most important requirements of a four-wheel drive vehicle is absolute reliability. Your vehicle should, therefore, be in top shape and should be checked thoroughly by a qualified mechanic and auto-electrician each time you head into the wilds. You should also familiarize yourself with all the routine maintenance tasks that should be carried out in the bush. Make a point of regularly checking the chassis, suspension, differential and gearbox for defects.

What to take

To travel in the wilds you will have to be self-sufficient in respect of all your needs for the trip. What you take along will depend on the duration of the trip, time of year, accommodation and amenities available along the route and the size of the group.

On a long trip the first rule you should adhere to is to distinguish between essential, useful and luxury items to take along. Don't overload the vehicle as you will be putting it under unnecessary strain in difficult terrain and high temperatures. This can cause overheating and a host of other problems which are best avoided. Getting an overloaded vehicle unstuck is also far more difficult than a lighter vehicle.

Topping the list of essentials are spares, equipment and tools. Long stretches of the routes described in this book follow tar or well-maintained gravel routes that are often used by other motorists. Here you won't need to carry the full range of spares (*see* Checklist opposite), but once you head into remote areas a comprehensive range of spares is vital. Carry at least two spare wheels and tyres. A highlift jack is very useful, but if not used correctly it can be dangerous and even lethal – ensure that the moving parts are well oiled and free of dirt, otherwise the jack could malfunction. Also essential is a radiator screen to prevent grass seeds from accumulating in the radiator. Other spares, equipment and tools you should have are listed in the Checklist.

Equally important are fuel and water. If your vehicle is not fitted with a long-range tank, store additional fuel in jerry cans. Ensure that they do not leak and cannot bounce around. Water containers must be clearly distinguishable from fuel containers.

No matter how good your vehicle's service record is, a breakdown in the bush at some stage or other is inevitable. Ideally, you should have some mechanical knowledge, but, even if you are not mechanically minded, you might be able to trace and repair a fault if you have a good book on car repairs and maintenance and a repair manual. A well-equipped tool box is essential.

Except for South Africa and Namibia where, with a few exceptions, the rest camps are fenced, rest camps and campsites in other Southern African conservation areas are generally unfenced and animals often pass through campsites at night. Some species, like hyenas, are attracted by the possibility of finding food, making it dangerous to sleep in the open. A good tent with a sewn-in ground sheet is essential. Other vital pieces of camping gear include a strong light (gas or rechargeable battery) and a durable torch with a strong beam for each member of your party.

The winter months are generally the best to explore most of Southern Africa, the only exceptions being the winter rainfall region of the Western Cape and the all-year-round rainfall region of the Western and the Eastern Cape. Bear in mind that winter days can be cool, especially in highland areas, while temperatures of close to freezing point are not uncommon during the night and early mornings. In summer light clothing will suffice, but you should have waterproof rain gear handy for the afternoon

Above: *When travelling to remote places, vehicles must be fitted out with all the necessary equipment and spares.*

thunderstorms. Long-sleeved shirts and long trousers will help to lessen the chance of being bitten by mosquitoes.

Two sets of clothing, in addition to what you are wearing, are usually sufficient for trips of up to seven days. For longer trips you can make adjustments accordingly. A sunhat is essential, even in winter, while a tracksuit is suitable for both daytime and at night. Keep a set of spare clothing for more formal occasions.

Home comforts add to the enjoyment of the bush and after a long, hot dusty drive a few days into your trip an ice cold beer, cooldrink or a crispy salad is much appreciated. While a good-quality coolbox can serve you well for up to four days, a freezer is essential for long and frequent trips into the bush. This will be an expensive investment and you would be well advised to read the specifications of the various products carefully. Aspects to consider include the temperature range of the fridge/freezer in relation to the ambient temperature at which this was calculated, its capacity and whether it is battery or gas operated.

Before heading for the bush, ensure that there is a supply of extra food and water on board, should you become stranded. Your spare rations must be sufficient for at least five days and should be stored away from goods meant for daily consumption. Don't be tempted to use them under normal circumstances.

When you are travelling in a group of two or more vehicles, it makes sense to divide equipment so that the load can be kept down. This leaves more space for non-essential equipment which adds to the pleasure of life in the bush. For large parties it might even be worthwhile to use a backup vehicle to carry spares, tools, fuel and non-essential equipment.

There are few things as frustrating as discovering that crucial equipment has been left at home. When packing, use a checklist and pack systematically to ensure that all essentials are packed first. Bush-wise travellers have their own packing methods, but we find that the easiest way to keep track of things is to use different coloured plastic crates – one for breakfast, one for lunch, one for supper and two for cooking and eating utensils. With a little practice you will soon know where everything fits.

CHECKLIST

IMPORTANT TO REMEMBER
Compass or GPS
Emergency food and water
First aid kit
Knife
Maps
Permits
Spare food and water
Travel and vehicle documentation
 (where required)

SPARES AND EQUIPMENT
Axe
Brake fluid
Coil (depending on type of ignition)
Condensor (depending on type of
 ignition)
Distributor cap (depending on type
 of ignition)
Electrical wire, 5 m length
Engine/gearbox mountings
Exhaust repair kit
Fan belt/s
Fire extinguisher
Fuel filter
Fuel pump kit
Funnel
Fuses
Glue, epoxy or quick-set adhesive
Grease
Hose clamps
Inner tubes
Insulation tape
Jack, high-lift and bottle
Jerry cans
Jumper cables
Light bulbs
Main leaf spring set, shackle hangers,
 bushes and pins
Moisture repellant
Oil, engine and gearbox
Points or spare electric ignition
Puncture repair kit
Radiator cap, hoses and clamps
Shock absorbers, set
Snatch rope
Spade
Spare keys
Spark plugs
Spare wheels x 2 complete
Tow rope
Tubes, valves and valve caps

Tyre pressure gauge
Tyre pump
Tyre repair kit
Water pump

TOOLS
Chisel
Feeler gauge (if required)
Files, flat and round
Hacksaw and blades
Jack, high-lift
Hammer, small and 1,8 kg
Nuts, bolts and washers to fit main
 attachment points
Pliers, longnose, circlip and fencing
Repair manual
Screwdrivers, set of flat head and
 Phillips
Socket spanner set and accessories
Spanners, set of flat and ring (8 mm
 to 21 mm), shifting
Spark plug wrench
Tyre levers
Wheel spanner
Wire
Wire cutters
Wrench, monkey

CAMPING EQUIPMENT
Brush or small broom
Chairs
Cord, 5 m thin nylon
Folding table
Light, gas or battery operated
Mattress
Pillow
Sleeping bag
Space blanket
Tarpaulin
Tent (with built-in groundsheet)
Tent pegs and poles

COOKING
Braai grid
Can opener
Cooking utensils
Coolbox (or fridge)
Cutlery
Detergent
Dishcloth
Dishwashing liquid
Firelighters

Food
Gas bottle and cooker top
Matches
Plates, cups, etc.
Pots, heavy-duty flat pot, 'driebeen
 potjie' and frying pan
Pot-scourer
Refuse bags, heavy duty
Spare jets (for cooker top)
Water containers

CLOTHING
Boots or comfortable walking shoes
Jersey
Rain gear, waterproof
Shirts, long- and short-sleeved
Shorts
Sleepwear
Spare clothing
Spare footwear (for evenings)
Socks
Sunhat
Swimming costume
Tracksuit
Trousers
Underwear

PERSONAL
Cash and credit cards
Brush or comb
Insect repellent
Lip salve
Moisturizer
Shampoo and conditioner
Shaver
Soap
Sunglasses
Sunscreen
Tissues
Toilet paper
Toothbrush and toothpaste
Torch and spare batteries
Towel

MISCELLANEOUS
Binoculars
Camera
Field guides and reference books
Film
Notebook
Pen/pencil
Tripod (for camera)

Hints and rules for an enjoyable bush experience

Disrespect for the bush and poor planning can easily turn a dream holiday into a nightmare. The following are just a few basic common sense rules and hints which you should adhere to at all times.

● The most important aspect of any four-wheel drive tour is proper planning. Obtain as much information as possible in advance about destinations by studying topographical maps, as well as maps obtainable from automobile associations and tourist information bureaux. Also read as much as you can about the countries and destinations to be visited.

● Before setting off on your tour, have your vehicle checked thoroughly to ensure that it will get you where you are heading and back. In remote areas spare parts are often unavailable and the money spent on a service or check-up beforehand could save you a lot of time and frustration.

● Ensure that you have the necessary permits, the correct travel and vehicle documentation and that you comply with all health requirements when your tour involves cross-border travelling.

● Inform someone of your planned route, destination and dates and do not deviate from your route, unless forced to do so by circumstances. In the event of a breakdown, remain with your vehicle – especially in big-game areas.

● Always carry emergency food and water that will last at least five days, as well as a comprehensive range of spare parts.

● Remain well within the load capacity of your vehicle. When packing, ensure that the vehicle is not top-heavy or carrying too much weight on the rear axle.

● Keep a constant check on the weather forecast, especially during the rainy season, and avoid travelling and sleeping in river valleys. Flash floods can occur with little warning.

● Enquire regularly about road conditions ahead from those most likely to be able to give you accurate information.

● When travelling in remote areas, check the availability of fuel at destinations ahead of you and carry sufficient fuel to get you to the next refuelling stop. Remember to take enough cash as garages in remote areas accept only cash.

● Do not rely on getting to your destination by chance – being lost and disoriented is certainly no joke. Always carry a set of detailed maps and refer to them regularly to ensure that you are on the right track.

Opposite: The Naukluft 4x4 Trail offers magnificent views.
Above: The puff adder is responsible for more cases of snake bite than any other species.

● When you are visiting the wilds, you should always be aware of potentially dangerous animals such as predators, elephant, rhino, lone buffalo and snakes, especially at night.

● Reduce your speed on gravel roads – hitting a pothole at 100 km/h could put an end to your holiday plans. Always switch on your lights when travelling behind a vehicle on a gravel road, also when overtaking and when approaching oncoming traffic.

● When anticipating difficult driving conditions, engage four-wheel drive before you get yourself into trouble. In soft loose sand, deflate tyre pressure to about 1 Kpa (front) and 1,2 Kpa (rear). Although this is time-consuming, tyres should be reflated to the recommended pressure once you are back on tar or gravel.

● Never cross a river unless you are able to wade through it. The current might be too strong, or there might be obstacles or washaways that could get you into serious trouble. If a river is fordable, approach it slowly and accelerate gradually to increase your speed. This will create a wall of water in front of the vehicle. Increase power output when the water gets deeper or resistance increases, but do so gently. As a general rule, try to cross where the river starts running across the road.

● On steep descents, engage four-wheel drive low range, first gear, and take your feet off the petrol and clutch pedals, allowing the vehicle to crawl along against its engine revolutions.

● Rocky terrain and steep ascents should be negotiated slowly and with caution. Be especially aware of the position of low points underneath the vehicle. Engage four-wheel drive low range, first gear, and ease the vehicle over obstacles, rather than using brute force. Tyres should be hard, but not over-inflated.

● Avoid driving at night, unless absolutely necessary. Domestic and wild animals, especially kudu, are difficult to see.

Maps

When planning a trip, good maps are essential – even more so when you leave the highways. For general use on proclaimed public roads the maps published by the Automobile Association of South Africa are highly recommended. The AA's travel service publications include detailed maps of each province with tourist information and touring maps of specific routes (for example Johannesburg/Pretoria to Beit Bridge). Also available is a series of reference and through-route maps with detailed central area and through-route maps of the major centres.

The AA of South Africa also publishes road maps of Botswana and Zimbabwe. Road maps and maps of Zimbabwe's national parks are obtainable from the offices of the AA of Zimbabwe in Harare, Bulawayo, Gweru and Mutare. Useful for travelling in Namibia is the AA of Namibia's road map, as well as the map compiled by the Department of Transport, available free of charge. Maps published by the AA of South Africa, Namibia and Zimbabwe are available free of charge to members of the AASA, and some of the AASA services are also available in neighbouring countries.

Highly recommended for travelling in Botswana is the Shell tourist map of that country. Drawn to a scale of 1:720 000, it has 270 GPS co-ordinates with map references and 12 enlarged maps of tourist destinations. Shell has also published excellent maps of Chobe National Park and Moremi Game Reserve.

Maps of Zambia and Mozambique are notoriously difficult to obtain. The best general purpose map of Mozambique (map no. 6821) is published by Ravenstein to a scale of 1:2 000 000. For topographical maps, contact the Department of Maps and Land Attribution (DINAGECA) in Maputo (see page 172).

Problems can occur when you leave the highways as the quality of some road maps of Southern Africa is poor and 'secondary' roads could turn out to be non-existent tracks. Do not be misled by the colour or width of the roads on maps. In some instances secondary roads and four-wheel drive tracks may be indicated in the same line strength.

Poles used for road signs are highly sought after as building material in rural areas and a problem frequently encountered by travellers in Southern Africa is the absence of road signs where they are most needed. Obtaining directions can be equally frustrating. Ask anyone: 'Is this the road to...?' and there is a good chance that the response will be 'Yes', even if you are 180 degrees off course. The advantage of having a good map and being able to use it in such situations is obvious – it will save you lots of time, frustrations and unnecessary travelling.

Topographical maps are by far the most detailed and reliable. Available in scales of 1:500 000, 1:250 000 and 1:50 000, they have details of all topographical and artificial features. Bear in mind, though, that the numerous tracks that are blazed by prospectors, local inhabitants and irresponsible off-road drivers are not indicated on these maps. Although extremely useful, it is usually impractical to have a full set of 1:50 000 maps of a long route – here the 1:250 000 maps will be much more practical. For the addresses of where these maps can be obtained, see Useful addresses and telephone numbers on page 172.

A map alone is of little value, especially in dense woodlands and featureless terrain where there are very often no landmarks, and you should therefore familiarize yourself with map-reading techniques and the use of a compass. Practise your skills, starting in familiar terrain and moving gradually into unfamiliar terrain until you are confident enough to travel far off the beaten track.

A good habit when travelling in unfamiliar terrain is to get your co-driver to draw a map, with odometer distances, as you are travelling. If you get lost or have to backtrack, finding your way back will be far easier. In addition, the map can be used at a later stage when you would like to explore an area further.

Getting accurate information about the condition of roads can be frustrating. In some parts of Southern Africa distances and road conditions are relative terms. What is considered by some to be a good road, often turns out to be a mere track. You will be well advised to obtain such information from reliable sources such as government officials, aid workers, non-governmental organizations and also the police. It is especially important to have the right information during the rainy season when large areas could become impassable.

A very useful piece of equipment, especially when you get that gnawing feeling of being totally lost, is the GPS, or Global Positioning System. This compact navigation aid uses a sophisticated system of 24 satellites in orbit 20 000 km above the earth. Your position is calculated by the GPS receiver, which measures the time that it takes to receive radio signals from at least three satellites. Since the system is operated by the United States Department of Defence, its accuracy can be manipulated during war. A good receiver is usually accurate to within 15 m.

The GPS can also show you exactly where you have been and where you are going. Waypoints along a route can be entered before you set off and the receiver will then provide up-to-date information about the distance, bearing and estimated time en route to each waypoint.

While this is an exceedingly useful piece of satellite navigation wizardry, it should preferably be used only as a back-up to your own navigation skills. It is especially comforting when you are in doubt or lost, or need to get to a destination that is difficult to reach using conventional navigation skills. Over-reliance on a GPS can, however, easily cause you to pay so much attention to the display screen that you cannot appreciate the scenery, or it could tempt you to blaze your own trail, simply because of the direction indicated on your display screen.

Opposite: *The Swartberg range creates a formidable barrier between the Little Karoo and the Great Karoo.*

Staying healthy in the bush

While the most common ailment in the bush is likely to be an overdose of sun, accidents and serious medical situations do, unfortunately, occur. They could arise when you are hundreds of kilometres from the nearest assistance, making it essential to carry a good first aid kit and, above all, to know how to use it. Ideally, a member of your party should be trained in first aid. You should at least have a copy of *The South African First Aid Manual*, the authorized manual of St John Ambulance and the South African Red Cross Society, or any other good manual.

One of the reasons for the existence of wild places is the fact that they are usually unsuited to permanent human habitation, often for health reasons. Malaria is currently the greatest health threat in Southern Africa; not only are risk areas expanding, but there is increasing resistance to some drugs, especially Chloroquine. Before entering any malarial area a doctor must be consulted to obtain prophylactic drugs that are suited to the area you are visiting. In Zambia, for example, resistance has been reported to Chloroquine, Fansidar and Mefloquine.

Bear in mind that prophylaxis is no guarantee against malaria; it is important to take other protection measures to reduce the risk of contracting the disease. Precautions include sleeping under a mosquito net, applying a mosquito repellent to exposed skin and wearing long-sleeved shirts and long trousers at night.

Symptoms usually show up after about two weeks and, as they are similar to flu, malaria is often not identified immediately. If fever, sweating, body ache, headache, nausea, diarrhoea and vomiting occur, consult a doctor at once – it is very important to point out that you have visited a malarial area.

Another disease that is still rampant in large parts of Southern Africa is bilharzia, which is caused by a parasite that attacks the intestines, bladder and other organs of humans and animals. It is often prevalent in water bodies near human habitation and as a general rule you should avoid swimming or washing in water near or downstream of human settlements. Also avoid pools of stagnant or slow-moving water. Symptoms include weariness, a high temperature and blood in the urine and faeces and can take up to six weeks to develop. Although it is not a life-threatening disease, you should consult a doctor as soon as possible.

In South Africa, Botswana, Namibia and Zimbabwe it is considered safe to drink the water in cities, towns and tourist areas, as well as most rural areas. In Zambia and Mozambique, however, you would be well advised to drink only bottled water, even in Lusaka and Maputo. When at all in doubt about the quality of water in rural areas, it is best to boil it for a few minutes. Fresh food should, likewise, be treated with caution.

Despite a protracted campaign against the tsetse fly, it has not been eradicated entirely. It is still widespread in Zambia and sporadic outbreaks occur in other areas from time to time. It is a yellowish to brownish fly, slightly larger than the common house fly, with scissor-like wings.

While the incidence is not high, a bite from an infected tsetse fly could result in sleeping sickness (trypanosomiasis). Symptoms include an inflamed bite site, swelling of the lymph glands and bad headaches. Should any of these symptoms occur, you should consult a doctor as soon as possible. Preventative medication is not available for this disease, but the chances of being bitten can be reduced by wearing trousers and long-sleeved shirts in dull colours – tsetse flies are said to be attracted to bright colours.

Although tick-bite fever is seldom fatal, it should be treated seriously and medical advice should be sought at the earliest opportunity. The symptoms usually develop within seven to ten days and include fever, swollen glands, severe headache, body ache and tiredness. The risk of being bitten can be reduced by wearing trousers and a long-sleeved shirt. Alternatively, clothes can be sprayed with tick repellent or washed in an emulsifiable concentrate that repels biting insects. A thorough body check should be made after walking through grass and scrub. If a tick has already attached itself to the skin, it should be removed as soon as possible. The best way is to burn it with a lighter or a match. Also effective is to cover it with an oily substance – this will starve it of oxygen, causing it to release its grip.

Prevention is better than cure; sunburn and heat exhaustion, spider, scorpion and snake bites can be avoided by following a few basic rules. Apply lots of sunscreen and keep your water intake high. Be careful when collecting wood or picking up rocks – spiders, scorpions and snakes often use these as their home. Although most snakes will usually avoid confrontation, this is not the case with the puff adder, the snake responsible for most snake bite deaths in Southern Africa. When walking in the veld, always be on the lookout for snakes – step onto rocks, not over them, and look carefully before putting your feet down.

In the event of a serious medical emergency, evacuation might be necessary. It is, therefore, highly recommended that you take out medical insurance and membership of a medical emergency service. Medical Rescue International (MedRescue) provides a 24-hour service throughout South Africa, as well as in Namibia, Botswana, Zimbabwe, Swaziland, Lesotho and Mozambique. In Zimbabwe, a medical emergency service is also rendered by Medical Air Rescue Service (MARS). A full range of medical services is offered by Specialty Emergency Services (SES) in Zambia. This not only includes evacuation, but SES will also provide information on the location of doctors, hospitals, etc. (*see* Useful addresses and telephone numbers, page 172).

For travelling in remote areas, where medical supplies could be in short supply, it is advisable to take a sterilized needle kit along with you, in case you should need to receive an injection. This will also reduce the risk of HIV infection.

Opposite: *The Orange River provides a cool and refreshing retreat for visitors to the Richtersveld.*

✚ FIRST AID KIT

Antibiotic: broad spectrum

Anaesthetic: local spray-on for stings/bites

Malaria tablets

Anti-diarrhoea tablets

Needle and thread

Anti-histamine cream and tablets

Painkillers: mild and prescribed

Anti-inflammatory gel

Plaster: zinc oxide & elastoplast

Antiseptic cream and solution

Safety pins

Bandages: wide crepe and narrow gauze

Scissors

Cotton wool

Sling

Cough mixture

Splints

Dressing: wound and adhesive strips

Sunscreen cream: use a cream with a minimum protection factor of 12

After-sun treatment cream

Eardrops: antiseptic analgesic

Surgical gloves

Eye bath

Thermometer

Eyedrops

Throat lozenges

Gauze swabs

Tweezers

Insect repellent

Wound dressing

Indigestion tablets

Rehydration powder

Lip salve

Southern Africa's conservation areas

Nature has endowed Southern Africa with great riches and the sub-continent is host to a multitude of game species, birds, plant life, reptiles, butterflies and several smaller creatures that are quite easily overlooked. No less diverse than its wildlife is its scenery – a beautiful mosaic of lakes, rivers, waterfalls, vast salt pans, towering mountains, beaches, forests, woodlands and a fascinating array of geological formations.

Fortunately, much of the sub-continent's wildlife heritage and many of its unique natural attractions enjoy the protection of conservation; in some instances this has been the case for over a century. The primary objective of conservation is to manage these areas so that they will be preserved in their natural state.

Conservation is, however, also for the benefit of people and, in addition to wildlife management, conservation authorities are also involved in tourism. Each of the conservation authorities within the sub-region has adopted different approaches to the planning and establishment of tourist facilities. As a result, the type of facilities and the standard of accommodation varies considerably throughout the sub-region.

This section of the book provides a broad overview of the various conservation authorities and the facilities visitors can expect. It is of the utmost importance to ensure that you know exactly what equipment and amenities (such as cutlery, crockery and bedding) are provided when making a reservation as this will determine how self-sufficient you need to be and what equipment you should take.

The number of people visiting Southern Africa's parks and reserves has increased dramatically and, as a general rule, it is advisable to reserve accommodation well in advance. Until fairly recently it was possible to visit Botswana's parks without making prior reservations, but advance bookings are now required. Although obtaining permits might appear restrictive to some, it does ensure that parks are not overrun by hordes of people, thereby preserving their wilderness atmosphere.

BOTSWANA

About 17 per cent of Botswana enjoys conservation status as national parks, game reserves or forestry areas. The magical Okavango Delta is undoubtedly the country's main attraction and nearly a third of the Delta is protected within the boundaries of the Moremi Game Reserve with its large herds of game.

Contrasting sharply with the waterways and reed-lined channels of the Delta are the vast saline pans of Makgadikgadi and the savanna woodlands of the Central Kalahari Game Reserve. Home to one of the last remaining groups of the sub-continent's San people, the Central Kalahari is Africa's second largest conservation area.

Opposite: The floodplain grasslands of the Okavango Delta support large herds of buffalo.

To retain the wilderness atmosphere of the parks, tourist amenities are limited to basic campsites – these consist of a site to pitch a tent, a longdrop toilet and, if you are fortunate, showers. The only exception is Chobe Lodge in the Chobe National Park and a number of privately owned luxury camps in the Moremi Game Reserve. Visitors must, therefore, be self-sufficient in respect of all their requirements, including food. Unlike rest camps in South Africa's big game parks, the campsites are unfenced and potentially dangerous animals could be present at any given time.

LESOTHO

Situated on the Drakensberg escarpment in southeastern Lesotho, Sehlabathebe National Park is Lesotho's only conservation area. Its main attractions are the spectacular mountain scenery, strangely shaped sandstone formations, rock paintings and excellent trout fishing. Covering 6 805 ha, the park was proclaimed in 1970.

MOZAMBIQUE

Many years of civil war have destroyed much of Mozambique, including most of its wildlife heritage. The country is, however, slowly rebuilding its devastated infrastructure and the tourism industry is currently enjoying the attention of private investors as well as the government.

Nowadays most visitors to Mozambique are attracted by the superb scuba diving and other watersport opportunities off the Bazaruto Archipelago and the Mozambican south coast. Although much of the game in Mozambique's parks and reserves has been wiped out by poachers, the magnificent scenery and birdlife still makes a visit worthwhile. At the time of writing, Gorongosa National Park was about to be opened to specialist groups, such as birders, while Maputo Elephant Reserve was open to day visitors. Check with the Ministry of Flora and Fauna on the latest developments.

Visitors to Mozambique's parks should be totally self-sufficient, the only exception being the Bazaruto Archipelago which has a number of lodges.

NAMIBIA

Although most closely associated with the Namib Desert, Namibia offers a diversity of landscapes, including woodlands and the little-explored waterways of the Linyanti Swamps.

Namibia is one of the leading nations in conservation in Africa, with a history stretching back to 1907 when the first areas were set aside by the German administration for protection. Notable among the many successes of the country's conservation authorities is the preservation of the black rhino, and today Namibia is home to the largest population of this species in the world.

Namibia's 20 state-owned national parks, game parks and recreational resorts cover nearly 15 per cent of the country's surface. Flagship of the national parks is the Etosha National Park, while the Namib-Naukluft Park, with its majestic sand dunes and gravel plains, is becoming increasingly popular. Another well-known attraction is the Fish River Canyon, the second largest of its kind in the world.

The conservation function of the parks in Namibia rests with the Directorate of Resource Management of the Ministry of Environment and Tourism, while the management of the rest camps falls under Namibia Wildlife Resorts, a state-owned corporation. The rest camps and resorts are generally well run, accommodation is of a high standard and amenities at most rest camps include a restaurant, a well-stocked shop and a swimming pool. The parks in the northeast of the country (Khaudum, Caprivi, Mudumu and Mamili) are still undeveloped and the amenities here are limited to basic campsites with no facilities. The rest camps in these parks are unfenced, providing a true wilderness experience.

SOUTH AFRICA

Offering a variety of landscapes and wildlife experiences, South Africa is justifiably promoted as 'A World in One Country'. Within its borders are the expansive plains of the Karoo, the Cape Floral Kingdom, towering mountain peaks, vast tracts of bushveld and miles and miles of unspoilt beaches. It is recognized as a world leader in the field of conservation and counts among its parks two of the oldest conservation areas in Africa – Hluhluwe-Umfolozi and St Lucia. Among the many conservation successes are saving the white rhino, the bontebok and the Cape mountain zebra from extinction.

Unlike other Southern African countries where the management of wildlife is the responsibility of a single authority, this function in South Africa is shared by the National Parks Board and the respective provincial conservation authorities.

Established in 1926 by an act of Parliament, the National Parks Board is responsible for the conservation and management of a system of national parks representative of the country's ecosystems and unique natural features. By far the best known of the 17 parks (covering nearly 3,5 million ha) managed by the Board is the Kruger National Park.

Accommodation in South Africa's national parks is of the very highest standard, ranging from secluded bush camps and modern chalets to rustic rondavels and campsites with hot and cold water ablutions. All the rest camps have restaurants and well-stocked shops, while some also have a swimming pool and conference facilities.

In KwaZulu-Natal the management of parks and reserves is shared by the Natal Parks Board and the KwaZulu Department of Nature Conservation. Established in 1947 as a statutory body, the Natal Parks Board manages over 60 protected areas in the province, ranging from the 5-ha Doreen Clark Nature Reserve to the 260 000-ha Greater St Lucia Wetland Park.

A wide range of accommodation is available in the parks of KwaZulu-Natal, but only three of the Natal Parks Board's camps, namely Hilltop in Hluhluwe-Umfolozi Park, Giant's Castle Game Reserve in the Drakensberg and Ntshondwe in Itala Game Reserve, have restaurants. Depending on the type of accommodation, visitors to all other rest camps in the region must either do their own cooking, or make use of the services of the cook in attendance at some of the camps. A fairly limited range of basic food supplies is available from the shops in the Board's more popular rest camps. The Board is renowned for its high standards of accommodation and services as well as its wildlife management.

The KwaZulu Department of Nature Conservation manages the conservation areas in the former homeland of KwaZulu, among them the Ndumo Game Reserve, Tembe Elephant Park and the Kosi Bay Coastal Forest Reserve, including Lake Sibaya. Visitors must be self-sufficient in respect of all their supplies, as there are no shops in any of the Department's rest camps.

In the remaining eight regions of South Africa, provincial parks and reserves are managed by the conservation bodies of the respective provinces. The accommodation and visitor facilities in these game parks and nature reserves are usually of a very high standard.

SWAZILAND

Conservation is Swaziland is overseen by the Swaziland National Trust Commission. There are five conservation areas in the kingdom – one privately owned and the other four on state land. The privately owned Mlilwane Wildlife Sanctuary, established in 1960 by Terrence Reilly, is well stocked with game and offers a variety of activities. Malolotja Nature Reserve, with its magnificent mountain scenery, is regarded by many as Swaziland's most spectacular reserve. Accommodation at Malolotja consists of either camping or self-catering housing, and visitors must be self-sufficient. It is advisable to book accommodation well in advance for both parks.

ZAMBIA

Zambia's 19 national parks cover nearly eight per cent of the country's surface, while the 31 adjacent game management areas (GMAs) cover a further 23 per cent. Unfortunately, though, the country's wildlife heritage has suffered heavily as a result of more than a quarter of a century of poaching. The country was once the preserve of large herds of game, but it has been estimated that game numbers decreased by 80 per cent between 1970 and the early 1990s, while the black rhino has been exterminated. Years of neglect have also resulted in many rest camps falling into disrepair, while some were destroyed by the armed forces.

Do not let this deter you from visiting this beautiful country. There are still large herds of game and this, combined with an atmosphere of total wilderness and the isolation of some of the game parks, makes the country an ideal destination to explore in a four-wheel drive vehicle.

In addition, many positive developments are taking place. Government-owned lodges, camps and campsites are being leased to private entrepreneurs, which will result in vast improvements in accommodation and facilities. In some parks, game numbers are on the increase again, following the successful establishment of game management areas – multiple-use areas that serve as buffer zones between the parks and the more densely inhabited regions. These game management areas are zoned for purposes of wildlife utilization, such as controlled hunting, and are managed by the communities living in them.

Visitors to Zambia have to be self-sufficient in all respects, especially when travelling in the more remote areas.

ZIMBABWE

Zimbabwe's Parks and Wildlife Estate covers nearly 13 per cent of the country's surface. It includes national parks, recreational parks, safari areas, sanctuaries, botanical gardens and reserves.

These conservation areas offer a wide variety of contrasting landscapes, ranging from the scenic mountains of the Eastern Highlands to the woodlands in the west and the awe-inspiring Victoria Falls, undoubtedly the country's most famous tourist attraction. Hwange, Zimbabwe's most popular national park, is host to a variety of game, including thousands of elephants, while Mana Pools National Park offers some of the best game

viewing in Africa, especially between August and October, at the end of the dry season. Accommodation ranges from fully equipped lodges and cottages to chalets and campsites. Exclusive camps for one party each of up to 12 people are available at both Hwange and Matusadona national parks. Special camps with the bare minimum of facilities have been set aside in secluded areas of Mana Pools and Chizarira national parks. Check at the time of reservation what facilities are provided with the type of accommodation you have booked.

Unfortunately, the infrastructure of parks has deteriorated steadily over the past few years (even the country's flagship national park, Hwange, has not escaped), mainly as a result of the extremely small budgetary allocation to the conservation authority. To boost revenue, park fees were increased drastically in January 1997 and it is hoped that the increased income will be ploughed back into maintaining facilities and conservation.

Amenities at Hwange include a shop – stocked with basic food supplies – and a restaurant at each of the four camps, but visitors to all other camps should be self-sufficient. Also bear in mind that the rest camps and campsites in the big game areas are unfenced, except those in Hwange.

Below: *In winter the waterholes of Namibia's Etosha National Park provide a passing parade of animals.*

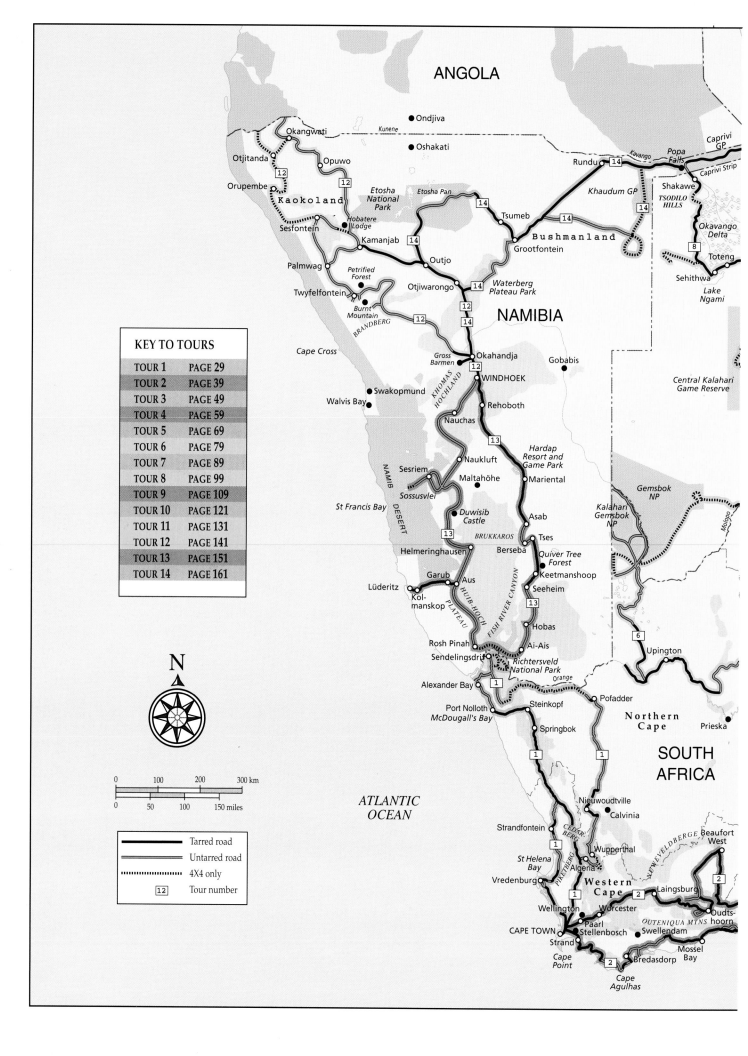

ANGOLA

• Ondjiva

• Oshakati

Kunene

Okangwati

Otjitanda

Opuwo

12

12

Orupembe

Kaokoland

Etosha
National
Park

Etosha Pan

Rundu

14

Kavango

Popa
Falls

Caprivi
GP

Caprivi Strip

14

Khaudum GP

Shakawe

14

TSODILO
HILLS

14

Tsumeb

14

Okavango
Delta

8

Sesfontein

Hobatere
Lodge

Kamanjab

14

Outjo

Bushmanland

Grootfontein

Toteng

Palmwag

Petrified
Forest

14

Otjiwarongo

14

Waterberg
Plateau Park

Sehithwa

Lake
Ngami

Twyfelfontein

Burnt
Mountain

12

12

12

NAMIBIA

BRANDBERG

Cape Cross

Gross
Barmen

Okahandja

14

Gobabis

Central Kalahari
Game Reserve

12

WINDHOEK

KEY TO TOURS

TOUR 1	PAGE 29
TOUR 2	PAGE 39
TOUR 3	PAGE 49
TOUR 4	PAGE 59
TOUR 5	PAGE 69
TOUR 6	PAGE 79
TOUR 7	PAGE 89
TOUR 8	PAGE 99
TOUR 9	PAGE 109
TOUR 10	PAGE 121
TOUR 11	PAGE 131
TOUR 12	PAGE 141
TOUR 13	PAGE 151
TOUR 14	PAGE 161

Swakopmund

Walvis Bay

KHOMAS
HOCHLAND

Rehoboth

Nauchas

13

Hardap
Resort and
Game Park

Naukluft

Sesriem

Maltahöhe

Mariental

Gemsbok
NP

St Francis Bay

Sossusvlei

NAMIB
DESERT

Duwisib
Castle

Asab

Kalahari
Gemsbok
NP

Molopo

13

Helmeringhausen

BRUKKAROS

Tses

Berseba

Quiver Tree
Forest

Garub

Aus

Keetmanshoop

Seeheim

Lüderitz

HUIB-HOCH
PLATEAU

FISH RIVER CANYON

13

Kol-
manskop

6

Upington

Hobas

Rosh Pinah

Ai-Ais

Sendelingsdrif

Richtersveld
National Park

Orange

Pofadder

Alexander Bay

1

Port Nolloth
McDougall's Bay

Steinkopf

Northern
Cape

Prieska

Springbok

1

1

SOUTH
AFRICA

N

Nieuwoudtville

Calvinia

0   100   200   300 km

0   50   100   150 miles

Strandfontein

1

CEDAR-
BERG

Wupperthal

HANTAMSBERGE Beaufort
West

2

ATLANTIC
OCEAN

St Helena
Bay

Algeria

PIKETBERG

Western
Cape

2

Laingsburg

2

Oudts-
hoorn

Vredenburg

1

Worcester

OUTENIQUA MTNS

Wellington

2

Paarl

Swellendam

Mossel
Bay

CAPE TOWN

Stellenbosch

Strand

Cape
Point

2

Bredasdorp

Cape
Agulhas

———— Tarred road

———— Untarred road

·········· 4X4 only

12 Tour number

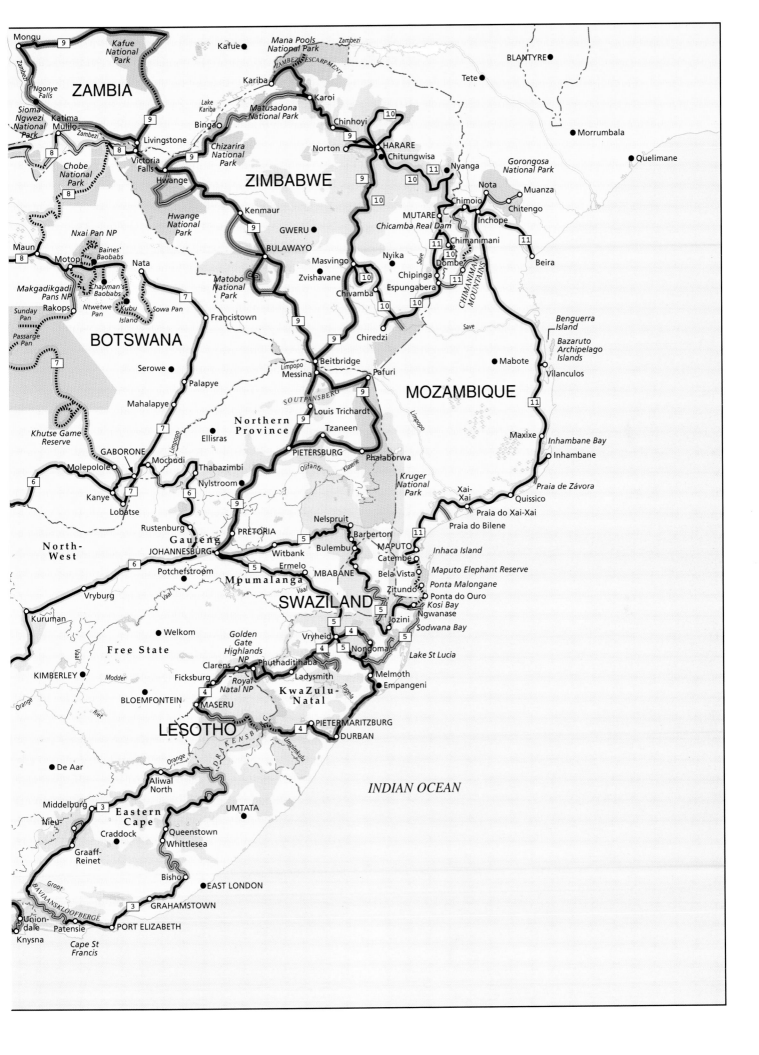

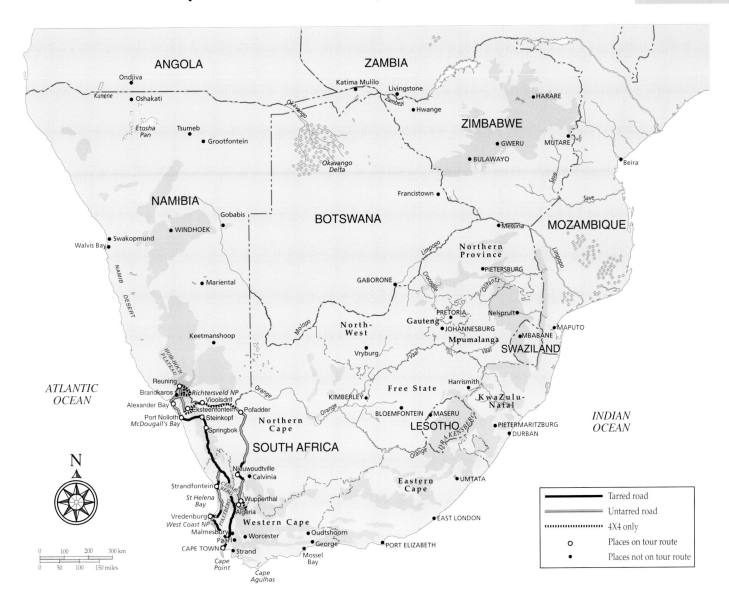

Starting in Cape Town, the Mother City, this tour covers the Northern Cape Province, an arid region dominated by open spaces. The area is especially beautiful during the spring flower season (usually early August to mid-September) when the barren landscape of Namaqualand is transformed into a floral carpet. The route of roughly 3 000 km takes about three weeks.

From Cape Town head north on the N7 through the wheat-producing Swartland towns of Malmesbury, Moorreesburg and Piketberg. Beyond Piekenierskloof Pass the wheatfields give way to citrus orchards and vineyards, cultivated on the fertile banks of the Olifants River, with the majestic Cedarberg dominating the scenery to the east. Take the signposted turnoff to Algeria, 26 km north of Citrusdal, onto a gravel road.

Opposite: *This whitewashed cottage at St Helena Bay is characteristic of the fishermen's cottages along the West Coast.*

ALGERIA

Situated beside the Rondegat River, Algeria is one of the main access points to the Cedarberg Wilderness Area. The 71 000-ha wilderness is home to the endemic cedar tree, snow protea and rocket pincushion, and is also a sanctuary to a small leopard population. Adding to the lure of the wilderness are craggy mountain peaks and natural rock sculptures. Among these are the Cathedral Rocks, the 30-m-high Wolfberg Arch (reminiscent of a memorial arch) and the 20-m-high Maltese Cross.

Algeria campsite, with its shady trees and well-kept lawns, is a starting point for day and overnight hikes. Self-catering accommodation is available at the foot of the old Uitkyk Pass.

From Algeria the route continues over the Cedarberg Pass and along the Driehoeks River Valley, bounded in the west by Sneeuberg – the highest peak in the Cedarberg. Prominent to the east are Sneeukop, Tafelberg and Wolfberg.

Above: The 30-m-high Wolfberg Arch is one of the best-known natural rock sculptures in the Cedarberg Wilderness Area.

SANDDRIF

Sanddrif, base for exploring the magnificent Wolfberg Cracks, is reached about 26 km beyond Algeria. Hemmed in by rock walls towering up to 30 m high, the main Crack cuts nearly a kilometre through the heart of the Wolfberg. Although strenuous, a climb is well worth the effort and can be extended to include the spectacular Wolfberg Arch. Ask for directions from the Nieuwoudts at Dwarsrivier farm.

Sanddrif has fully-equipped, self-catering chalets and camp-sites. Petrol is available at Dwarsrivier farm and you are advised to fill up here. The farm also has a small shop with basic groceries, frozen meat and firewood. Wine lovers should sample some of the good-quality white and red wines produced on Dwarsrivier.

WUPPERTHAL

After leaving Sanddrif, head for the well-known Elephant Cave on the 12 800-ha Matjiesrivier Nature Reserve. In addition to rock paintings of elephants, rows of human figures clad in karosses (skin garments) are also depicted. The nearby Stadsaal Caves are fascinating sandstone outcrops of orange rock carved by the elements into pillars, caves and passages.

At the reserve headquarters, take the gravel track heading northwest past the remote communities of Eselbank and Langkloof. The track descends quite steeply along a winding pass (take care when driving here) shortly before reaching Wupperthal, 35 km beyond Matjiesrivier.

Nestling in the Tratra Valley, the lush gardens of Wupperthal are in stark contrast to the bleakness of the surrounding mountains. Characterized by rows of whitewashed, thatched cottages, the settlement dates back to 1830 when the Rhenish Mission Society established a mission station here. The thatch-roofed church with its ornate Cape Dutch gable was inaugurated in 1835.

From Wupperthal the route continues over the Kouberg Pass and leads through the Biedouw Valley, worth exploring during the flower season. Travel along the Calvinia road towards the Nieuwoudtville turnoff, found beyond the Botterkloof Pass. The turnoff to the Oorlogskloof Nature Reserve is signposted 18 km south of Nieuwoudtville. The reserve has a wealth of flowering plants, but the only means of access is to follow the hiking trails meandering past interesting rock formations and caves with rock paintings. About 7 km before reaching Nieuwoudtville, be sure to stop at the Glacial Pavements, signposted 'Gletserspore' – deep grooves scoured into the rock by boulders caught up in glaciers some 300 million years ago.

NIEUWOUDTVILLE

Also known as the Boland of the Karoo, Nieuwoudtville lies on the edge of the Bokkeveld escarpment. This charming village has some attractive sandstone buildings (the imposing Dutch Reformed Church is a national monument) and is known for its outstanding display of spring flowers. Especially noteworthy is the variety of geophytes, among them vast fields of yellow bulbinellas. The Nieuwoudtville Wild Flower Reserve on the outskirts of town boasts over 300 plant species. Nieuwoudtville has a caravan park, hotel, filling station and shops.

Some 5 km down the Loeriesfontein road you will reach the turnoff to the Nieuwoudtville Falls. After rain the Doorn River plunges into a deep gorge – the spectacular waterfall is a sight not to be missed. About 25 km further you pass an unusually large concentration of quiver trees, known as the 'Kokerboomwoud' (Quiver Tree Forest). From Loeriesfontein the route traverses the sparsely vegetated Bushmanland plains, named after the San people who once lived there. To reach Pofadder, take the gravel secondary roads through far-flung settlements with peculiar names such as Granaatboskolk, Kraandraai and Houmoed.

POFADDER

Often referred to in jest as the archetype of a South African 'dorp', Pofadder lies within prime cattle country and is an important centre of the mining industry in the Northern Cape. Named after Klaas Pofadder, the chief of a clan of Korana, the town developed around a mission station established here in 1875. It is a good place to replenish supplies and fill up with petrol for the journey ahead.

NAMAQUALAND 4x4 TRAIL

The starting point of this 614-km route is the historic mission settlement of Pella near Pofadder. The rough trail varies between graded gravel roads, sandy river beds, canyons and winding mountain passes. To explore and appreciate the magnificent scenery at leisure, at least five days should be set aside for this part of the tour. Although rocky and at times demanding, the route is fairly easy for most of the way and is well signposted.

Accommodation in the area ranges from designated campsites to traditional Nama huts and private facilities.

The first section of the trail covers the 328 km between Pella and Viooolsdrif. The attractions of Pella, established by the London Missionary Society in 1814, include the Roman Catholic cathedral, old mill stones and date palm plantations.

The second section traverses the 248 km between Viooolsdrif (where you should fill up with petrol) and Brandkaros, 27 km from the diamond-mining town of Alexander Bay. A worthwhile excursion is to visit the Thumbprint – a rock formation with a classical anticlinal fold – situated close to the Peace of Paradise Camp. Also near the camp you will find some interesting rock engravings done by San people, depicting circles, spirals, stars and other abstract figures. The camp is an ideal base for the 50-km circular drive through the Helskloof Nature Reserve, a highly recommended outing for which a full day should be set aside. En route to Brandkaros, the trail passes through the quaint Richtersveld settlement of Eksteenfontein, where you will find a shop, bottle store and filling station (petrol only).

From Brandkaros it is a 66-km drive to Reuning, the head-quarters of the Richtersveld National Park. Along the way you could stop to view the rare bastard quiver trees on Cornellskop as well as the Wondergat, a sinkhole revered by the early Nama inhabitants as the lair of their deity, Heitsi Eibib.

Below: Namaqualand is home to over 4 000 plant species and in spring the usually drab landscape is transformed into a dazzling display of beautiful colours.

RICHTERSVELD NATIONAL PARK

The forbidding and mountainous landscape of the Richtersveld National Park belies the diversity of its succulents – the area boasts the richest variety of these plants in the world. One of the prime floral attractions is the intriguing elephant's trunk or *halfmens* which grows in clusters among the park's slopes, creating the impression of sentinels guarding their surroundings. Other prominent species include the bastard quiver tree and the maiden's quiver tree, the squat botterboom, flowering stones *(Lithops)*, vygies and plakkies.

The Richtersveld is a desert of ever-changing vistas – contorted mountains (with awe-inspiring names like Mount Terror and Devil's Tooth), narrow valleys, wide plains and rocks fashioned into bizarre shapes by wind, rain and extremes of temperature.

An unusual feature of this 162 445-ha park (proclaimed in 1991) is that the Nama inhabitants continue their traditional way of life here, which also involves stock-farming. The area is rich in reptiles (the Namib sand snake, southern rock agama and common barking gecko are just a few of the 52 species), while the bird list numbers almost 200 species, including the black eagle, Ludwig's bustard, swallowtailed bee-eater and mountain chat.

Below: The rugged and mountainous terrain of the Richtersveld, South Africa's only mountain desert, is ideally negotiated in a four-wheel drive vehicle.

The terrain is ideal 4x4 country, but, to prevent damage to the sensitive substrate, travel is restricted to a network of numbered routes, covering about 180 km. Accommodation consists of a choice of five designated campsites without any facilities.

ALEXANDER BAY

Alexander Bay, 7 km upstream of the Orange River mouth, was named after the British explorer James Alexander. He began mining copper in the Richtersveld in 1838 and conceived the ingenious plan of transporting the ore down the river on barges.

Following the discovery of diamonds along the Namaqualand coast, the coastal strip was proclaimed State Alluvial Diggings. In 1989 the mine and the entire town was transferred to a state-owned parastatal, Alexcor.

Set time aside for a tour of the diamond mine which includes a visit to lichen fields, the seal colony and the company's oyster farm. Otherwise visit the town's interesting mining museum.

PORT NOLLOTH

Southeast of Alexander Bay, Port Nolloth developed around the port and railhead built here in the late 1850s to export copper. Wooden houses imported from Denmark a century ago can still be seen. Today, Port Nolloth is the centre of the offshore diamond mining, lobster and white fish industries. Nearby McDougall's Bay is a popular holiday destination.

The Sandveld, the coastal strip between the Olifants and Orange rivers, is usually the first to change into its seasonal garb of spring flowers, transforming the landscape into shades of orange, yellow, white and red. Visitors can view the floral spectacle on the farms Kannikwa and Gemsbokvlei, off the Steinkopf road. Enquire at Top Wheel Motors in Port Nolloth.

STEINKOPF

Like many other Namaqualand villages, Steinkopf was founded as a mission station for the Nama people. The traditional 'matjieshuise' which used to characterize the village have largely been replaced by hessian and plastic material or brick structures.

SPRINGBOK

Lured by reports of rich copper deposits, Simon van der Stel undertook an expedition into the interior in 1685, hoping to discover Monomopata, an African kingdom in Zimbabwe famed for its wealth. The party camped a mere 5 km east of present-day Springbok and sank three prospecting shafts, the largest of which is now a national monument. When Van der Stel's scouting party failed to find a suitable site for a harbour, interest in the mining of copper waned. It was not until 1852 that the hills northwest of the town were exploited and the Blue Mine came into operation.

Relics of the early mining days include the Blue Mine (with its viewing platform), the smelter smoke stack in Springbok and the museum in the town's old synagogue that depicts the history and

Above: Goegap Nature Reserve, southeast of Springbok, is representative of the landscape and vegetation of the Namaqualand Klipkoppe.

development of Namaqualand. And no visit to Springbok is complete without viewing Jopie Kotze's extensive collection of rocks and minerals at the Springbok Lodge. Other mining relics in the region include the mining museum at Nababeep, and the Cornish beam pump and the adjacent smoke stack at Okiep. For more details, enquire at the information bureau in Springbok.

Spend a few days exploring the byways in the area, especially during the flower season. It is a good idea to check with the information bureau to find out where the best floral displays are. Within easy reach of Springbok is the Goegap Nature Reserve – 15 000 ha of typical Namaqualand vegetation and animal life. In addition to the normal tourist route, the reserve offers a scenic 4x4 route, as well as a mountain bike and horse trail.

The final leg of the return route to Cape Town follows the tarred N7 south for 562 km, passing Kamieskroon, Garies, Bitterfontein, Nuwerus, Vanrhynsdorp, Clanwilliam, Citrusdal and the Swartland. Although the drive can easily be done in about six hours, set aside an extra day or two during the spring flower season. Alternatively, you could return via the quaint West Coast villages of Strandfontein, Doring Bay, Lambert's Bay, Eland's Bay, Dwarskersbos and Paternoster, sampling some of the delicious crayfish along the way.

Left: *Like a lone sentinel, the 20-m-high Maltese Cross stands guard over the bizarre rock formations of the Cedarberg.*
Top: *In the more remote areas of the Cedarberg, donkey carts are still used as a form of transport.*
Above: *The shady campsites along the banks of the Rondegat River at Algeria are a popular weekend retreat.*
Following pages: *Flowing through the harsh, arid landscape of the Richtersveld, the Orange River is an unexpected and most refreshing sight to the weary traveller.*

Overberg Coast, Garden Route and Karoo

2

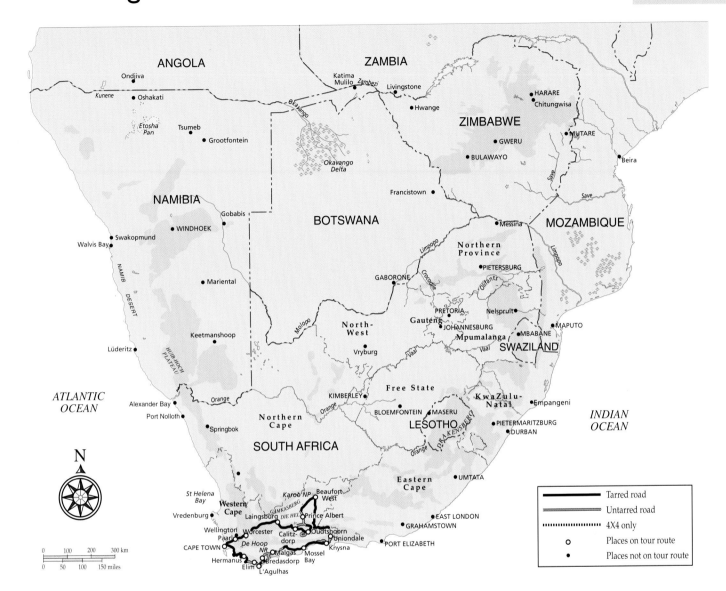

Starting in Cape Town, this route explores the coastal region of the Overberg, and continues to Cape Agulhas and the Garden Route. It then traverses the vast plains of the Great Karoo and the Little Karoo before heading back through the Hex River Valley and the Paarl winelands. About 60 per cent of the 2 000-km route, which can be completed in two to three weeks, is on tar, while 630 km is on gravel, making it possible to do most of the route in a sedan car. The three four-wheel drive sections cover 170 km.

Cape Town has a myriad of well-known tourist attractions, among the most popular being the Victoria and Alfred Waterfront, Table Mountain and the cable car, Kirstenbosch National Botanical Garden and the Cape of Good Hope Nature Reserve.

Opposite: *Folded sandstone strata in the Seweweekspoort bear testimony to the forces of nature that shaped the mountains of the southern Cape 100 million years ago.*

THE WHALE COAST

From Cape Town, the route cuts through the Cape Flats and then follows the winding coastal road through Gordon's Bay and Kleinmond to Betty's Bay. Here time can be spent walking to the waterfall in Disa Kloof in the Harold Porter Botanical Gardens, or visiting the Penguin Reserve at Stoney Point, one of only three mainland colonies of the jackass penguin in Southern Africa. Continuing along the Whale Coast, the route leads through Kleinmond to Hermanus, one of the 12 best land-based whale-watching sites in the world.

Up to 70 southern right whales migrate to the breeding and calving grounds of Walker Bay, near Hermanus, each year, September and October being the peak season. During the whale season, sightings are announced on Market Square by the only whale crier in the world. The cliffs hugging the coast provide excellent vantage points and the whales sometimes

Above: *The manually operated pont at Malgas is the only one of its kind in South Africa.*

approach to within about 10 m of the coast. While you are in Hermanus, visit the Old Harbour Museum to listen to the whale sounds, transmitted from a sonar buoy in the bay.

ELIM

As you leave Hermanus the next stop is the fishing village of Gansbaai from where the charming settlement of Elim can be reached via back roads. Founded by the Moravian Mission Church in 1824, Elim has typical Strandveld thatch-roofed cottages and its streets are lined with fig trees. The focal point of this settlement, which has been proclaimed a national monument in its entirety, is the sizable thatch-roofed church, dating back to 1835. The water mill has the largest wooden water wheel in South Africa. Built in 1833, it was restored in 1990 and produces stone-milled wheat for the bakery – try the bread!

L'AGULHAS

The route now follows back roads to the coastal resorts of Struisbaai and L'Agulhas. Built in 1848, the lighthouse at Cape Agulhas is the second oldest in the country and now houses the Lighthouse Museum. This museum is the only one of its kind in South Africa and it depicts the history and development of lighthouses through the ages.

Also worth visiting in the area is the much-photographed fishing village of Arniston, an enormous wave-cut cavern known as Waenhuiskrans, and the Shipwreck Museum in Bredasdorp.

DE HOOP NATURE RESERVE

To reach this reserve with its interesting diversity of habitats, follow the R319 from Bredasdorp and turn right onto a gravel road, continuing to the signposted turnoff.

Covering about 36 000 ha, De Hoop Nature Reserve has a large population of bontebok, while Cape mountain zebra, eland and grey rhebok also occur here. Several rare, endangered and endemic fynbos species grow in the reserve, including *Protea aurea* subs. *potbergensis* (long-bud sugarbush), *Protea denticulata, Aspalathus potbergensis, Polygala potbergensis* and *Roella rhodantha.* De Hoop Vlei is a wetland of international importance, while the cliffs of Potberg are home to the only breeding colony of the Cape vulture in the Western Cape. The coastline off De Hoop Nature Reserve is the most important breeding and calving ground of the southern right whale and during September and October it offers some of the best whale watching in the world. Day walks along De Hoop Vlei and at Potberg, as well as mountain bike routes, cater for the energetic.

MALGAS

On leaving the reserve, turn right, continue past Ouplaas and Wydgeleë and then take the Malgas road. Here you can enjoy the novelty of crossing the Breede River on the last manually operated pont in South Africa. The pont crossing at Malgas has been in use since September 1830. The present pont dates all the way back to 1914 and was operated for 27 years by the legendary Moxie Dunn.

On joining the R322, continue to the N2 and then on to Heidelberg, Riversdale, Albertinia, Mossel Bay and George.

KNYSNA

To reach Knysna from George, you have two options: either take the N2 through Wilderness and the Lakes District, or follow the Passes Road along the foothills of the Outeniqua Mountains. Set on the shores of a superb lagoon, with the forest-clad slopes of the Outeniqua Mountains dominating the scenery to the north, Knysna is one of South Africa's top holiday destinations. The Heads, two stone portals guarding the entrance to the lagoon, offer visitors a spectacular view of Knysna. Fishing enthusiasts will enjoy visiting the Angling Museum in the Old Jail Complex in Queen Street. One of only four such museums in the world, it depicts the history of angling and fishing methods in Africa. For a different perspective, take a cruise on the lagoon or visit the Featherbed Nature Reserve on the slopes of the Western Head.

PRINCE ALFRED'S PASS

From Knysna, travel eastwards for 4 km and turn onto the Prince Alfred's Pass road. One of the most scenic routes in the country, the road winds through impressive forests of yellowwood, stinkwood, ironwood and white stinkwood. Visitors can enjoy the tranquillity of the forest while picnicking at tables alongside the road, or stop at the King Edward VII Big Tree to admire this towering 39-m-high yellowwood. The Spitskop viewpoint offers beautiful vistas over the forests and the Knysna Lagoon in the distance. A short way on is the Valley of Ferns – a glade of verdant tree ferns in a magical setting.

The route now leads through the settlement of Kruisvallei to Die Vlug at the foot of Prince Alfred's Pass. For the next 13 km the road ascends steadily to the summit and then winds down to the Langkloof Valley.

Avontuur, at the western end of the valley, is a terminus for the 283-km-long narrow-gauge railway line which serves the apple farms of the Langkloof from Humewood in Port Elizabeth. (During the apple season a special train, the Apple Express, takes tourists on day excursions from Humewood Road to Lourie and back to Port Elizabeth.) Completed in 1907, it is the only narrow-gauge railway line in South Africa outside KwaZulu-Natal.

MEIRINGSPOORT

From Avontuur the route leads through the imposing Uniondale Poort to Uniondale and then via Buffelsklip to De Rust, a small farming settlement in the foothills of the Swartberg. The route now meanders through Meiringspoort, a narrow ravine carved by the Groot River through the Swartberg. Hemmed in by sheer orange cliffs with striking folds, the road crosses the river no less than 25 times. Along the route you pass Herrie se Klip, where the writer, C J Langenhoven, chiselled the name of his imaginary elephant, Herrie, into a rock. Further along, at Watervaldrift, you will reach the 60-m-high Meiringspoort Waterfall.

After you leave the Meiringspoort area, the Karoo – an arid region featuring endless plains, table-top mountains and cone-shaped 'koppies' – lies ahead. The region is well known for its Karoo lamb. The animals feed on the aromatic Karoo shrubs, known as 'bossies', which gives their meat a distinctive flavour.

KAROO NATIONAL PARK

Covering nearly 33 000 ha of dramatic Karoo scenery, this park is home to a variety of game, including springbok, gemsbok, Cape mountain zebra, red hartebeest, kudu, mountain reedbuck and klipspringer. It is also a sanctuary for the endangered riverine rabbit and the black rhino. A 13-km game-viewing drive takes you around the southwestern corner of the park, and a 3,5-km drive goes from the plains to the middle plateau along the Klipspringer Pass. To enable visitors to gain some knowledge of the flora and to savour the Karoo's distinctive atmosphere, two excellent walks have been laid out in the vicinity of the rest camp. Not to be missed is the Fossil Trail, a 400-m route with displays of fossils and information on the Karoo's geology.

The rest camp in the foothills of the Nuweveld Mountains offers accommodation either in thatched Karoo cottages or at camping sites. Other amenities include an information centre, restaurant, shop and swimming pool.

KAROO 4x4 TRAIL

The Karoo 4x4 Trail in the Karoo National Park was the first off-road route to be established in a South African national park. Covering 80 km over two days, the trail makes its way across a variety of terrain types and includes some challenging sections.

From the rest camp the route climbs steeply up Pienaar's Pass to the middle plateau and then winds along the slopes of the Nuweveld Mountains before descending to the overnight stop. Accommodation at Afsaal is provided in a restored shepherd's cottage, dating back a century. Facilities include a communal

Above: *Sweeping hairpin bends and dry-packed stone walls are characteristic of the dramatic Swartberg Pass linking the Little Karoo and the Great Karoo.*

sleeping area (mattresses are supplied but you should bring your own bedding), an outdoor braai area, drinking water and a toilet.

The second day's route initially traverses the plains and then ascends the slopes below the Nuweveld Mountains, following the previous day's route. From the middle plateau the trail winds down along the Klipspringer Pass to the rest camp.

SWARTBERG PASS

Leaving the park, the route to the Swartberg Pass follows the N1 past the railway station of Leeu Gamka and then heads south to Prince Albert, a charming village in the northern foothills of the Swartberg Mountains. Prince Albert has managed to retain much of its 19th-century atmosphere and among its numerous well-preserved buildings are typical Karoo cottages with their flat roofs and symmetrical facades, as well as several Cape Dutch, Georgian and Victorian houses. Also of interest is the old water mill, dating back to 1850.

The road now heads up the Swartberg Pass, one of the masterpieces of the great road builder Thomas Bain. After making its way through a narrow gorge at the northern gateway, the road coils upwards in a series of spectacular bends, revealing the hand-packed retaining walls – a technique used by the road engineer Andrew Geddes Bain (father of Thomas).

GAMKASKLOOF

Near the top of the Swartberg Pass a signpost indicates the turn-off to Gamkaskloof, also known as Die Hel. Until the completion of the road in 1963 this remote valley could be reached only on foot, and the small community lived in almost total isolation. They farmed there with goats, and also cultivated wheat, beans, grapes and fruit in the fertile soil. Drought, floods and other hardships eventually forced the people out of Gamkaskloof and in 1991 the last farmer left the valley. To conserve the cultural-historical heritage of Gamkaskloof, Cape Nature Conservation has initiated a conservation programme and some of the white-washed and thatched cottages have now been restored. Plans to establish a living museum are in the pipeline.

Backtrack to the Swartberg Pass, and proceed to the 1 585-m-high summit which affords visitors extensive views over the Little Karoo to the south, and the Swartberg Mountains and the Great Karoo to the north. On the way to Oudtshoorn, you can stop and explore the caverns and narrow passages of the magnificent Cango Caves. Other attractions in the area include the ostrich farms and the Cango Wildlife ranch (3 km outside Oudtshoorn) where crocodiles can be viewed. This is where the legendary Zindago, a large crocodile known to have killed two people, used to be the star attraction. Guided tours of the ranch, also famous for its cheetahs, are available.

GAMKA MOUNTAIN 4x4 TRAIL

Travel towards Calitzdorp and then along the Warmbad road to the signposted turnoff to the Gamka Mountain Nature Reserve. Covering 9 428 ha, the isolated mountain between the Swartberg and the Outeniqua Mountains was proclaimed a reserve in 1974 as a sanctuary for the Cape mountain zebra.

The Zebra Crossing 4x4 Trail covers about 60 km of rugged mountainous terrain. Tierkloof camp, at the start of the trail, provides tented accommodation equipped with beds, lamps, stove, fridge, braai facilities, firewood and ablutions.

From here the trail ascends steadily to Bakenkop, gaining over 700 m in altitude and then winding down to the overnight spot at Oukraal – a camping site with a fireplace, wood and a toilet. On the second day the route meanders to two splendid view-points on the edge of the plateau before returning to Oukraal. It then descends to the reserve's southern gate.

On leaving the reserve, take the Volmoed road and rejoin the R62, continuing through Calitzdorp to the historic mission settlement of Amalienstein. This settlement was founded in 1833 by the Berlin Mission Society as a breakaway congregation of the nearby Zoar Mission. Named after Amalie von Stein, a benefactress, the village is characterized by its quaint cottages, lush orchards and vineyards.

SEWEWEEKSPOORT

This scenic route follows the course of the Seweweekspoort River, which has carved a 15-km-long ravine ('poort') through the Little Swartberg Mountains. The views along the poort are impressive, with layers of sandstone that have been warped and twisted over the years into asymmetrical folds.

After winding over the Koueveld Pass, the route continues along a valley before ascending the Wit Nekke and the Rooinek Pass to reach the town of Laingsburg. Matjiesfontein is about 27 km beyond Laingsburg, situated just off the N1. Established in 1883 as a health resort, Matjiesfontein became an important refreshment stop for passing trains in the 1880s. The focal point of this charming Victorian village is the Lord Milner Hotel and the Laird's Arms.

HEXVALLEI 4x4 TRAIL

After travelling through the arid Karoo landscape, you will encounter the patchwork of vineyards in the fertile Hex River Valley, which rates as one of the most beautiful sights in South Africa. In winter the Hex River Mountains are often snow-capped, enhancing the panorama that unfolds as the road winds down into the valley with its more than eight million grape vines.

The Hexvallei 4x4 Trail traverses two private farms in the Hex River Valley. The route starts at the foot of the Quadu Mountains and then follows the old ox-wagon trail to the north. Along the way trailists will enjoy magnificent views over the valley, the Karoo and the Koo Valley – renowned for its apples – to the south. The 30-km route takes about three hours, but visitors can overnight in the De Hoop cottage.

Once back on the N1, it is a 90-minute drive back to Cape Town through Worcester and along the old Du Toitskloof Pass to Paarl. Alternatively, if you take the 4-km Huguenot Tunnel, it reduces the distance by 11 km, but this means missing out on the scenic splendour of the old pass. A visit to Paarl Mountain, a large granite dome dominating the skyline above the town, is rewarded with splendid vistas of the surrounding winelands. Call in at the publicity association to obtain details of the Paarl Wine Route, and make sure you leave enough time to sample some of the excellent wines produced in the area.

Opposite: *Pumpkins of all shapes and sizes are the speciality of this farm stall just outside Worcester.*

Above: *Fynbos sweeps down to the Atlantic coast along the scenic Clarence Drive stretching between Gordon's Bay and Rooiels.*

Right: *Protected by the Knysna Heads, the Knysna Lagoon is popular with watersport enthusiasts. It is also home to the intriguing sea-horse.*

Top: The spectacular Cango Caves in the bowels of the Swartberg are a fairytale world of stalagmites and stalactites.

Above: The malachite kingfisher can usually be seen perched on branches or reeds just above the water. It is one of five kingfisher species occurring in the Wilderness Lakes area.

Right: Visitors to the Karoo National Park, just outside Beaufort West, are accommodated in comfortable thatched chalets reflecting the building style used in the Karoo by the pioneers.

Following pages: In winter the peaks towering above the fertile Hex River Valley with its millions of vines are often capped in snow.

Eastern Cape

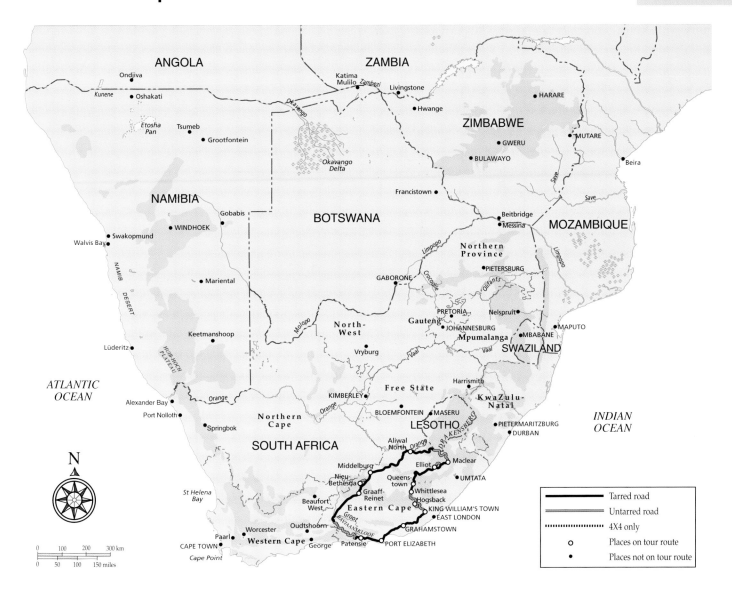

3

Starting in Port Elizabeth, this tour of just under two weeks explores the Eastern Cape and southern Drakensberg. Although much of the 2 100-km route is on tar, it takes in some of South Africa's least explored areas. Except for the Osseberg 4x4 Route and the Bastervoetpad, a four-wheel drive vehicle is not required and the route can be negotiated in a vehicle with a high ground clearance and even in a sedan car. In winter heavy snowfalls in the high mountains can make the roads impassable for days.

PORT ELIZABETH

The main attraction of this popular seaside city with its sweeping white beaches is the Oceanarium, where the dolphins and seals have delighted millions of people with their performances. The

Opposite: *The scenic Katberg Pass winds through grassland, plantations and beautiful indigenous forests.*

Oceanarium has underground viewing windows (enabling visitors to observe the dolphins under the water) and an aquarium. A snake park, a tropical house with exotic plants and birds, and a museum with maritime displays all form part of the complex. The best way to see the city's numerous historic buildings is to set off on the Heritage Trail, a 5-km walk.

From Port Elizabeth the route follows the N2 westwards for 40 km to the Gamtoosmond and Lourie offramp. Winding along the fertile Gamtoos Valley, the road passes the settlements of Lourie, Hankey and Patensie and, 16 km beyond Patensie, a rock formation that resembles the profile of Queen Victoria.

OSSEBERG 4x4 ROUTE

The turnoff to the start of this trail is 41 km beyond Patensie. From there it is another 4,5 km to the start, where you will find a campsite with a communal braai area and ablution facilities.

Above: Euphorbias are conspicuous in the valley bushveld vegetation of the Baviaanskloof – a valley so wild that it qualifies as a wilderness area.

Covering about 20 km, the route initially follows the course of the Groot River, which has chiselled a 450-m-deep gorge through the sandstone. Due to the sheer cliffs, mottled with colourful lichens, the route crosses the river several times.

At Sandrivier, where the river makes a tight U-bend, the track takes a shortcut and then begins its tortuous ascent. It gains about 300 m in altitude to Rondekop before the gradient eases as it climbs to Withoogte. Dominating the scenery to the north are the Groot Winterhoek Mountains and the Cockscomb, named after its five crests that resemble a rooster's comb.

The route takes two to three hours to complete, depending on the level of the river. Vegetation ranges from valley bushveld at the start and acacias along the river bank to grassveld on the plateaux and grassy fynbos in the mountainous areas. Animals include bushbuck, kudu, mountain reedbuck, grey rhebok and baboon. From the end of the 4x4 route, you follow a farm road for a few kilometres until it joins the scenic road along the Elands River Valley. Head south for about 16 km to the junction with the R332 to Willowmore from where you retrace familiar ground back to the turnoff to the 4x4 route.

BAVIAANSKLOOF

Bounded by the Baviaanskloof Mountains to the north and the Kouga Mountains to the south, Baviaanskloof is a 170 000-ha wilderness of lichen-encrusted sandstone cliffs, deep ravines and rushing streams. Patches of indigenous forest survive in the kloofs, while aloes, cycads and euphorbias thrive on the valley slopes. The higher mountains are covered in fynbos, the plateaux in grasslands, and the western reaches of the range are home to the endemic Willowmore cedar. Game species include the Cape mountain zebra, kudu, eland, klipspringer, mountain reedbuck and grey rhebok, and the area has a rich diversity of birds.

The Grootrivier Poort, a magnificent gorge carved by the Groot River, is the eastern gateway to this scenic valley which extends westwards for 160 km to Willowmore. The road snakes through the forested gorge for about 10 km and then emerges into the secluded Goede Hoop Valley, the starting point of the Osseberg 4x4 Route (*see* page 49).

Some way further, the road crosses numerous streams as it winds along four passes, offering stupendous views of the surrounding country. Visitors can camp at several designated sites, obtain accommodation in the restored farmhouse at Doornkraal, or stay in the self-catering chalets at Geelhoutbos. Some of the recreational activities available include hiking, canoeing, angling, birding, mountain biking and swimming.

GRAAFF-REINET

From Willowmore it is an easy drive to Graaff-Reinet, the 'Gem of the Karoo'. Visit the publicity association and plan on a stay of at least two days. Established in 1786, Graaff-Reinet is the fourth oldest town in South Africa and has more national monuments than any other town in the country. Lining the streets are over 200 historic buildings – Victorian villas, whitewashed Karoo cottages and graceful Cape Dutch mansions. Among the striking buildings are the Reinet House (old parsonage), the Drostdy (old magistracy) and Stretch's Court, where freed slaves once lived.

Complementing the town's fine architecture is the magnificent scenery of the 16 500-ha Karoo Nature Reserve which virtually surrounds the town. Situated in the reserve is the awe-inspiring Valley of Desolation, a conglomeration of buttresses and rock pillars rising up to 120 m above the valley floor. From viewpoints in the vicinity you can enjoy panoramic vistas of Graaff-Reinet in the horseshoe-bend of the Sunday's River, the cone-shaped Spandaukop (3,5 km southeast of the Valley of Desolation) and Sneeuberg (about 55 km to the north of Graaff-Reinet).

NIEU-BETHESDA

Time has stood still at this remote village in the foothills of the Compassberg. Once almost forgotten, the tiny hamlet – with its water furrows and its streets lined with pear trees – was elevated to stardom when Athol Fugard's play, *The Road to Mecca*, was filmed here. Centre of attraction is the bizarre Owl House, a fantasy world of sculptures created by Miss Helen Martins. Regarded by most as eccentric, but by some as a genius, she committed suicide in 1976 by drinking caustic soda. Owls stare from the verandah, and the Camel Yard at the back of the house is crammed with more than 300 cement and glass sculptures – animals, giant birds and humans in various postures.

Top left: Owls in all shapes, colours and sizes are a dominant theme in the Owl House at Nieu-Bethesda.
Above: In winter the red and orange flowers of aloes brighten up the landscape of the Eastern Cape.

From Nieu-Bethesda, the route goes along a back road to the N9 which takes you via Middelburg, Steynsburg and Burgersdorp to Aliwal North, famous for its hot springs. Lady Grey, nestling in a valley between the Witteberg and Spioenkop, lies 53 km east of Aliwal North. Continue to Herschel, the birthplace of Olive Schreiner (author of *The Story of an African Farm*), and Sterkspruit. Descend from the Witteberg over 2 226-m-high Lundin's Nek to Moshesh's Ford and then travel eastwards to Rhodes.

RHODES

Cradled in a hidden valley of the Bell River, Rhodes is a charming settlement with a cluster of houses set among tall pine trees and blessed with invigorating mountain air. To the north the scenery is dominated by the 3 001-m-high Ben Macdhui, the highest point in the Cape Drakensberg. For most of the year Rhodes is serene, but after the first snowfalls it becomes the 'Switzerland of South Africa' and hordes of people flock to Tiffindell to ski on the slopes below Ben Macdhui.

NAUDÉSBERG PASS

The drive from Rhodes follows the Bell River Valley eastwards and then ascends the Naudésberg Pass in a series of sweeping curves. Near the summit, travellers come across a most unusual sight – a sheep kraal boasting a telephone booth which provides a link to the outside world for those trapped in the snow. Two kilometres further you reach the summit, at 2 500 m the highest pass in South Africa that is negotiable by sedan car. Verdant green in summer, golden-yellow in autumn and brown in winter, the hills below stretch endlessly into the hazy distance.

For the next 8 km the road descends steeply to the foot of the pass, losing nearly 600 m in altitude. The route now traverses undulating grassy hills where sheep and cattle graze peacefully, and further along crosses the Potberg Pass to reach Maclear.

DINOSAUR FOOTPRINTS

At Oakleigh farm, 16 km from Maclear, a 3-km detour leads to the site of the oldest dinosaur tracks in South Africa. Preserved in rock, the tracks are estimated to be about 200 million years old. In addition to the tracks of a small three-toed dinosaur, the tracks and the tail drag grooves of a large four-footed dinosaur can also be seen.

BASTERVOETPAD

From Maclear the route goes west to Ugie, a small farming settlement in the shadows of the spectacular Prentjiesberg with its fairytale sandstone rock turrets and pinnacles. Continuing further, the road passes Gatberg, an intriguing peak with an enormous hole just below its summit, and then reaches Elliot.

The route now ascends the scenic 8-km-long Barkly Pass, passing white sandstone outcrops and eroded rock formations. At the Mountain Shadows Hotel, just beyond the summit of the pass, take a short detour to the Kransies viewpoint which offers visitors a bird's-eye view of the valleys far below.

The turnoff onto the Bastervoetpad is immediately opposite the Mountain Shadows Hotel. About 20 km beyond the turnoff the road reaches the 2 240-m-high edge of the escarpment. From here you will have expansive views of the deep valleys, separated by steep grassy ridges, and creamy-white sandstone outcrops hundred of metres below. The descent is initially steep, losing some 400 m in altitude over the first 5 km. The road then winds along the slopes below Mount Enterprise, descending into a deep valley and crossing a river several times. About 19 km from the summit, turn right and continue along the Noah's Ark road, which meanders past Gatberg and Mount Ararat, before joining the tar road 20 km east of Elliot.

KATBERG PASS

From Elliot the route continues westwards to Indwe, a centre for the surrounding cattle and sheep farms, and then reaches the town of Dordrecht in the northern foothills of the Stormberg. Heading in a southwesterly direction, the road winds through Xhosa territory and, after crossing over Bongolo Nek, descends to Queenstown. It then continues past Whittlesea to Sada.

About 40 km from Sada lies an exposed sandstone outcrop, Devil's Bellows Nek, a well-known landmark on the Old Katberg Pass. From here the road winds down the scenic Didima Mountain, an outlier of the Winterberg range. Beautiful indigenous forests and green pine plantations hug the well-watered southern slopes. The Katberg Hotel, at the foot of the Pass, is a popular base for walks, horse-riding and cycling.

HOGSBACK

After passing through Balfour, the next town you will encounter, head for Seymour and take a leisurely drive along Michel's Pass to the mountain paradise of Hogsback. Set amidst verdant pine plantations and lush indigenous forests, the tiny hamlet takes its name after the triple peaks resembling the bristles on a hog's back. Forest walks lead to the many nearby waterfalls, and you can also go on a two-day hiking trail. Explore the numerous art and craft studios in the vicinity, or try to be there in October for the annual Hogsback Arts Festival. While each season has its own attractions, Hogsback is especially attractive in spring when thousands of azaleas and rhododendrons burst into bloom. It is also famous for its variety of berries (brambles, blackberries, loganberries, gooseberries, strawberries, Booysen berries and red, white and black currants) which are in season between December and February.

KEISKAMMAHOEK

Head down Hogsback Pass to the grasslands in the foothills of the Hogsback mountains and then east through Middeldrift. A short way beyond Middeldrift turn left to Keiskammahoek, a fertile basin bounded in the north by the Amatola Mountains. The slopes are clad in magnificent patches of indigenous forests of yellowwood, lemonwood, knobwood and assegai trees.

The tranquil rural scenery belies the area's turbulent history, and lonely memorials and battlefields are a silent testimony to the battles fought here during the 19th century. Between 1779 and 1853 eight frontier wars were fought in the Eastern Cape between the Xhosa and the British. These wars were caused by competition for grazing resources, land and the military actions of the British colonial government. Along the loop road, graves of British soldiers and Xhosa chiefs are reminders of these wars.

From Keiskammahoek the route continues over Red Hill Pass to Amalinde, where one of the region's bloodiest battles was fought between two rival Xhosa chiefs in 1818. A short way on is the Ntaba ka Ndoda Shrine, a monument to Xhosa chiefs who died in battle against the British.

After passing through the industrial town of Dimbaza, you will reach King William's Town. Among the many places worth exploring here is the Kaffrarian Museum with its large mammal collection. It also has an excellent ethnographic section on the Xhosa and Koisan people. The Missionary Museum focuses on the role of early missionaries in Southern Africa.

The homeward journey to Port Elizabeth leads through Settler Country to the historic town of Grahamstown. With over 40 churches, it is also known as the 'City of Saints'. The town has fine examples of Victorian and typical Eastern Cape houses, museums and numerous historic sites worth exploring. Perched on Gunfire Hill above Grahamstown is the 1820 Settlers National Monument, venue of the Standard Bank National Arts Festival, a showcase of South African art which is held in July each year. The remainder of the journey is an easy drive on the N2 back to Port Elizabeth.

Above: The bottlenose dolphins of the Port Elizabeth Dolphinarium have delighted thousands of people with their performances.
Below: Hogsback's 'Piggy' signs guide trailists along the network of footpaths meandering through the indigenous forests.
Right: Hogsback is blessed with an abundance of water, giving rise to tranquil streams, cascades and waterfalls.

Left: *From a viewpoint high above Graaff-Reinet, visitors can enjoy awe-inspiring views of the Valley of Desolation and Spandaukop.*
Top: *Port Elizabeth's long white beaches are popular with both watersport enthusiasts and sunbathers.*
Above: *The abundant nectar of the aloe is relished by the Xhosa people of the Eastern Cape.*
Following pages: *The tracks in the mountains above Rhodes in the Eastern Cape are best negotiated in a four-wheel drive vehicle.*

55

Drakensberg, Maloti Mountains and Battlefields

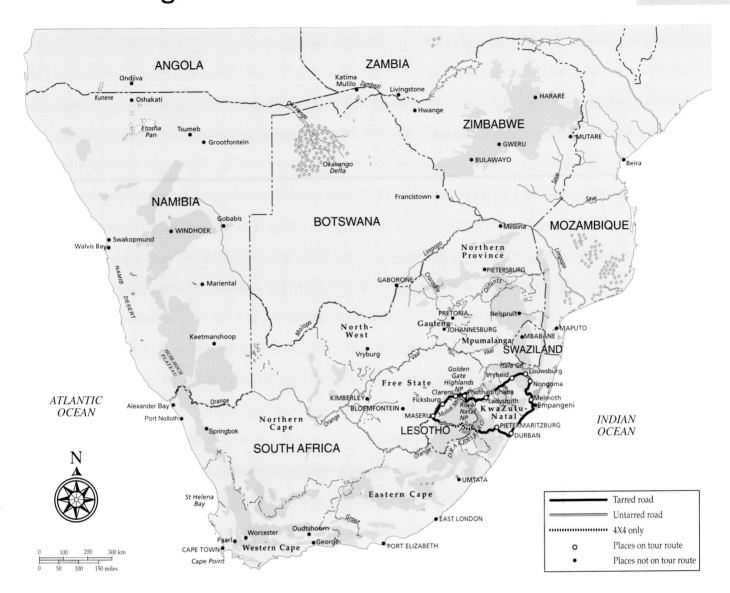

4

Sweeping vistas across the hills of the KwaZulu-Natal Midlands and the rugged scenery of the majestic Drakensberg and Maloti Mountains make this tour spectacular. After traversing the scenic highlands of Lesotho and the northeastern Free State, the tour follows the KwaZulu-Natal Battlefields route, returning to Durban across the hills and valleys of Zululand. The 2 200-km journey takes approximately two to three weeks to complete.

Very careful planning is required for the Lesotho Mountain road section of this tour, as the area is often covered in snow in winter. In summer, heavy thunderstorms occur which can create extremely difficult driving conditions and can flood causeways. It is therefore essential that this section of the tour is undertaken in a four-wheel drive vehicle.

Opposite: *Sani Pass is a formidable challenge to drivers, despite improvements made since it was pioneered in 1948.*

PIETERMARITZBURG

From Durban, take the N2 to Pietermaritzburg, also known as the Heritage City. It has a distinctly Victorian character, with fine old buildings, museums and parks. Among its 39 national monuments are City Hall, the old Natal Parliament buildings, old Supreme Court, and Publicity House, where tourist information on Pietermaritzburg and the Midlands can be obtained.

Continue through the farming district of Bulwer to Underberg and Himeville, quiet villages with superb views of the southern Drakensberg. Be sure to visit the craft shops along Sani Saunter, enjoy some flyfishing and stock up on petrol and supplies.

SANI PASS

From Himeville the route ascends Sani Pass, the only road into eastern Lesotho from KwaZulu-Natal. Once a footpath used by the San, Sani Pass became a pack mule route in 1931. However, it was not until 1948 that the route was attempted by a vehicle. After clearing immigration at the South African border post, take the track that twists steeply in a series of spectacular loops and U-bends to the Lesotho border post, 8 km further. With its summit at 2 874 m, Sani Pass is the highest mountain road in Southern Africa. Sani Top Chalet provides rustic self-catering accommodation and is a welcome stop after the taxing drive.

EASTERN LESOTHO

The route now continues in a northwesterly direction. From the Kotisephola Pass, the visitor will enjoy splendid views of the 3 482-m-high Thabana Ntlenyana (The Little Black Mountain), the highest point south of Mount Kilimanjaro. Descending into the Sehonghong River Valley, the remote village of Mokhotlong, 50 km beyond Sani Pass, is reached. Mokhotlong ('Place of the Bald Ibis'), the administrative centre of the district, consists of government buildings, a hospital, a few shops and a small hotel.

From Mokhotlong take the A3 leading through Rafolatsane and Molumong, then ascending steadily through montane grasslands to Thaba Phafane (3 250 m), where the Menoaneng Pass has to be negotiated. A tortuous ascent follows to the Senqu River, where the headwaters of the Orange River have chiselled a valley of a kilometre deep into the heart of the mountains.

A low-level causeway crosses the Senqu River at Koma Koma, but during the summer months when the river flows strongly it might be impassable. Should this be the case, your best option is to backtrack to Mokhotlong.

Below: *The Sentinel, or Brandwag, rock formation in the Golden Gate Highlands National Park rises 130 m above the Little Caledon River Valley.*

THE TRANS-MALOTI TRACK

The remaining 180 km of the route is a roller-coaster ride up steep mountain passes and down into deep river valleys. Only the steep inclines and declines from Cheche's Pass westwards are tarred, but from Molimo Nthuse the road is fully tarred.

Along the way you will pass remote settlements, and you will often encounter Basotho herdboys and horsemen wrapped in colourful blankets, as well as heavily laden buses transporting people to remote villages. As the buses crawl along, music blares over loudspeakers, warning waiting passengers and oncoming traffic of their approach.

From Koma Koma Bridge the track winds steadily up the eastern slopes of the Central Range to Thaba Tseka, crossing several small rivers. Fuel is available at the Fraser's Store here, but there is no tourist accommodation at Thaba Tseka.

The Basotho people have been a nation of horse riders since 1830 and their ponies are renowned for their hardiness. Visitors can ask to be shown around the Basotho Pony National Stud which was established at Thaba Tseka in 1978.

From Thaba Tseka, the road ascends steeply up Mokhoabong Pass (2 860 m) to the alpine grasslands of the Central Range. It then winds down to the Mantsonyane River Valley and the settlement of Mantsonyane. For the next 6 km the road snakes upwards to the 2 560-m-high summit of Cheche's Pass, only to lose 700 m in altitude as it descends to Marakabei in the valley of the Senqunyane River. Marakabei has a Fraser's lodge.

After another steep ascent the road contours around a mountain, with views of the deep valley to the north, and then drops to the Likalaneng Valley. Winding along the Likalaneng Pass up the eastern slopes of the Thaba Putsoa range, it reaches the 2 620-m-high summit of the Blue Mountain Pass.

The next obstacle, Molimo Nthuse Pass, is reached a short way on. Also known as 'God Help Me Pass', Molimo Nthuse marks the end of the gravel road. The Basotho Pony Trekking Centre, which organizes pony trekking trips into the mountains, is situated here. A popular day trek will take visitors to the Qiloane Falls, but overnight trips are also conducted. Nearby Molimo Nthuse Lodge is set amidst a grove of poplar, willow and wattle trees in the Makhaleng River Valley.

The road then gains 320 m to the summit of the Bushman's Pass (2 226 m), which offers splendid views of the Lesotho Lowlands to the west. A detour to Ha Baroana (Home of the Little Bushmen) will reward explorers with one of the largest of the estimated 5 000 rock painting sites in Lesotho. Depicted on the rock walls are eland, hartebeest, lion and human figures.

Further west, a turnoff is reached to Thaba Bosiu, Lesotho's most important historical site. From this stronghold, King Moshoeshoe I, founder of the Basotho nation, warded off several attacks by marauding tribes and an assault by Boer forces. Guided tours, lasting two to three hours, are conducted to the summit of the mountain fortress. Visitors can view the remains of the village, including the house where Moshoeshoe died and the graveyard where he and other chiefs were buried.

Return to the A3, heading west to Maseru, the capital of the Mountain Kingdom. Maseru is a small, bustling city with several handicraft shops where mohair tapestries and rugs, pottery, basketware, knitwear and leatherware can be bought.

CHERRY ROUTE

From Maseru the route continues through the cultivated fields of the Lowlands, with the Berea Plateau prominent to the east, to Teyateyaneng. Known as TY, the village is renowned for its pottery as well as its tapestries and rugs in mohair and karakul.

Leave Lesotho at the Peka Bridge border post to reach Ficksburg, centre of South Africa's Cherry Route. About 95 per cent of the country's cherries are produced in the area, which is really beautiful in September when the trees blossom. Visitors stream to Ficksburg in November to enjoy the annual Cherry Festival.

Beyond Ficksburg, the road skirts the Witteberg Range before reaching Fouriesburg, a small town overlooked by the Rooiberg Mountains. Amid undulating grasslands, the road follows the broad valley of the Caledon River with its poplar and willow trees. To the east the scenery is dominated by the sheer cliffs of the Front Range of the Maloti Mountains.

CLARENS

Situated in a basin formed by the Rooiberge, the picturesque village of Clarens is surrounded by green meadows punctuated by dramatic sandstone outcrops, buttresses and sheer cliff faces. Several artists have made Clarens their home, and the town has a variety of arts and crafts shops. Farms in the area cater for those seeking tranquillity or wanting to explore the region on foot or horseback. Many rock art sites and fossils can also be seen here.

GOLDEN GATE HIGHLANDS NATIONAL PARK

This park covers 11 630 ha of some of the most magnificent mountain scenery in South Africa. Sandstone buttresses soar skywards from the floor of the Little Caledon River Valley, while herds of antelope graze peacefully on the grassy slopes. The cliffs are home to the rare bearded vulture and the bald ibis.

Above: Streams lined by poplar and willow trees and white sandstone outcrops characterize the landscape around Clarens.

Visitors can explore two circular loop roads by car, set off on one of the splendid day walks, a two-day hiking trail or guided horse trails, a night drive or a visit to the vulture restaurant. They can also undertake a guided walk to the impressive Cathedral Cave with its dome-shaped roof.

Accommodation ranges from hotel-style rooms and self-catering bungalows at the Brandwag complex to self-catering stone cottages and campsites at nearby Glen Reenen Rest Camp.

QWAQWA NATIONAL PARK

Continuing eastwards along the Highland Treasure Route, the 22 000-ha QwaQwa National Park adjoins Golden Gate. Game known to have occurred in the area has been reintroduced and among the species to be seen here are black wildebeest, blesbok, eland, red hartebeest, Burchell's zebra and springbok.

Four-wheel drive adventurers will enjoy the three off-road trails, ranging from an easy route for novices to a more challenging trail to the summit of QwaQwa Mountain. Each takes two to three hours to complete, but they can be integrated into one. Facilities at the overnight stop consist of a sandstone hut equipped with ten double bunks and mattresses, a kitchen, flush toilets and an outside braai. Although this is not essential, groups are usually accompanied by a guide. The trail is closed in summer. For those wishing to explore the area on foot, try the 27-km overnight hiking trail. Self-catering accommodation is available at Eerstegeluk, a beautiful restored farmhouse west of the road to Kestell, while rustic accommodation is also provided.

Some 30 km east of Golden Gate, you reach the Basotho Cultural Village, a living museum which portrays the history, culture and lifestyle of the South Sotho. Weaving, traditional pottery and basketry demonstrations and a divination session by a traditional doctor provide a fascinating insight into the way of life of the South Sotho people. Visitors can also join a guided two-hour Herbal Trail, focusing on the uses of plants, go on a pony ride, or sit down to a traditional Basotho meal.

WITSIESHOEK PASS AND SENTINEL DRIVE

Phuthaditjhaba, formerly the capital of the homeland of Qwa-Qwa, is reached a little further. Take the mountain road out of town and after 19,9 km you will reach a tollgate. The road then passes underneath sandstone overhangs as it snakes its way up to the Witsieshoek Mountain Resort. Situated at 2 286 m above sea level, the resort is said to be the highest in Southern Africa and offers magnificent views over the Royal Natal National Park. From here the Sentinel Drive winds along a ridge for 6 km to the base of Sentinel Peak, departure point for hikes to the top of the Amphitheatre. Without doubt one of the most impressive sights in the Drakensberg, the Amphitheatre stretches for 5 km between the Sentinel and Eastern Buttress, its 500-m-high sheer rock wall forming a dramatic backdrop to the Royal Natal National Park.

Backtrack to Phuthaditjhaba, rejoin the Harrismith road and turn onto the Bergville road which winds past Sterkfontein Dam and down the Oliviershoek Pass to the Royal Natal National Park. Set against the majestic backdrop of the Amphitheatre, the park is criss-crossed by 25 walks and trails. Don't miss the Gorge Walk with its dazzling views of Eastern Buttress and the Devil's Tooth, the 65-m-long Tugela Tunnel and the Amphitheatre.

BATTLEFIELDS ROUTE

From here, travel via Bergville to Ladysmith on the Battlefields Route. Northern KwaZulu-Natal was once the theatre of many bloody battles, and during the 19th century names like Ladysmith, Isandlwana and Rorke's Drift made world headlines.

Among the places you may choose to visit is the Talana Museum at Dundee, situated on the site of the first major clash in the Second Anglo-Boer War (1899–1902). Rorke's Drift, scene of a fierce battle between 139 British troops and 3 000 to 4 000 Zulu impi on 22 January 1879, lies to the southeast of the town. Another well-known battlefield in the area is Isandlwana where 20 000 Zulu annihilated a force of 867 British soldiers and 900 Natal Native Pioneer Corps members. At the Blood River battlefield, where the Voortrekkers fought the Zulu in 1838, the site of the Boer laager is demarcated by bronze replicas of ox wagons.

ZULULAND

From Vryheid, continue to the Itala Game Reserve just north of Louwsburg. Situated on the Pongola River, this splendid reserve covers 29 653 ha of rolling hills, dissected by deep river valleys. Itala is home to a rich diversity of game, including black and white rhino, elephant, tsessebe, eland, giraffe, impala, blue wildebeest and reedbuck. Leopard and cheetah also occur there.

The reserve's rest camp, Ntshondwe, nestles among bush and rocks in idyllic surroundings. Amenities include a superb restaurant overlooking a waterhole, a swimming pool and a small shop. Itala also has a bush lodge, three bush camps, a small campsite and picnic sites. Visitors can tour the reserve by taking the Ngubhu Auto Trail, a 30-km circular self-drive trail, or by joining a guided morning or night drive. Early morning game-viewing walks are supervised by a game guard, while overnight trails are conducted between March and October.

From Louwsburg, head towards Ngome and turn left at route R618, continuing to the Ntendeka Wilderness Area with its forests, ferns and epiphytic orchids. Campsites are available, and a network of day walks allows you to explore the area.

Proceed to Nongoma and Ulundi where Cetshwayo established his capital, Ondini, in 1873. In the final battle of the Anglo-Zulu War, Cetshwayo was defeated here by a British force in 1879. Worth visiting is the site museum, a reconstruction of part of the original capital. The road then passes Umgungundlovu, the Great Kraal of the Zulu king, Dingane.

No visit to Zululand is complete without experiencing the Zulu culture. Visit Simunye, a traditional lodge south of Melmoth, or Shakaland with its authentic re-creation of Shaka's Great Kraal.

DURBAN

After you join the N2 just north of Gingindlovu it is a 115-km drive back to Durban along the Dolphin Coast. Popular holiday resorts dot the coastline, among them Zinkwazi Beach, Salt Rock, Ballito and Umhlanga Rocks.

With its Oriental atmosphere, Durban offers an insight into the Hindu and Muslim cultures. Be sure to visit the bustling and colourful Victoria Street Market and the Juma Mosque, the largest mosque in the southern hemisphere. Also worth visiting is the aquarium (renowned for its dolphin shows) and the snake park on the Golden Mile – Durban's holiday playground. The beaches here are safe for swimming, and the ricksha rides are popular.

Opposite: Fruit sellers displaying their wares at an informal roadside market near Empangeni in KwaZulu-Natal.
Above: The Blood River Monument is a reminder of the many battles fought in Zululand during the 19th century.
Right: The culture and history of the South Sotho people is portrayed at the Basotho Cultural Village.

Left: The sheer basalt wall of the Amphitheatre is one of South Africa's most impressive sights. It is flanked by the Eastern Buttress (left), Devil's Tooth and the Inner Tower.
Above: The Amphitheatre forms an imposing backdrop to the cottages at Tendele Camp in the Royal Natal National Park.
Following pages: The Free State is characterized by vast stretches of grasslands and maize fields. In winter the high-lying peaks are very often capped in snow.

Swaziland and Zululand

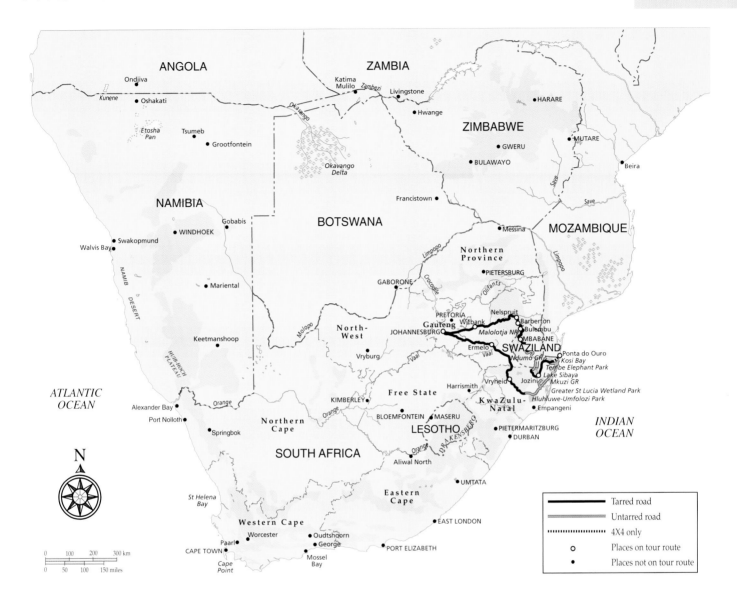

5

Ranging from the mountain scenery of Swaziland to the wildlife roaming the game reserves in Zululand and the pristine beaches along the Maputaland coast, this tour highlights some of the area's top attractions. Except for the four-wheel drive sections to Ponta do Ouro, Tembe Elephant Park, Kosi Mouth and the Ozabeni section of the Greater St Lucia Wetland Park, the 2 700-km route, lasting about four weeks, can be undertaken in a vehicle with a high ground clearance and even in a sedan car.

JOHANNESBURG

Also known as *eGoli*, Johannesburg is a vibrant city: the commercial capital of South Africa and heartbeat of the country's

Opposite: *The hides in the Mkuzi Game Reserve offer visitors an opportunity to view game at close quarters, among them blue wildebeest and Burchell's zebra.*

economy. It is a city of contrasts – poverty and affluence, shacks and skyscrapers, a mixture of African and Western cultures.

The top attraction just outside Johannesburg is without a doubt Gold Reef City, an authentic replica of Johannesburg during the hectic gold rush years of the late 1880s. Also worth visiting are the various museums in and around Johannesburg, most notably MuseumAfrica with its excellent cultural displays. To experience township life, jazz and a shebeen, consider a guided tour of Soweto.

BARBERTON

From Johannesburg take the N12 to Witbank and travel along the N4 to Nelspruit, where you can explore the lovely Lowveld National Botanical Gardens. The route continues southwards to the historic gold-mining town of Barberton where several house museums portray life in Barberton during the 1890s and the

Above: The Swazi people are highly skilled in a variety of handicrafts such as basketry and other grasswork.

early 1900s. Other relics of the gold-mining era include the façade of the first stock exchange in South Africa and the Lewis and Marks Building, dating back to 1887.

Covering about 2 km, the Fortuna Mine Trail on the outskirts of the town is a pleasing walk. You will need to take a strong torch as the route incorporates a 600-m tunnel, built in 1907 for the transportation of gold-bearing ore to the crushing mill.

The road to Swaziland continues along the Saddleback Pass to the Josefsdal/Bulembu border post. Along the route visitors will be able to see the cableway linking the Havelock Mine in Swaziland to the terminal in Barberton.

SWAZILAND

A short way beyond the border post is the village of Bulembu with its view of the Havelock Asbestos Mine, the largest of its kind in the world. The road now winds through eucalyptus and pine plantations to the small village of Pigg's Peak, where you can browse at the handicraft market and visit the weaving school.

Travel south on the King Mswati II Highway and cross the Komati River en route to the Malolotja Nature Reserve with its lovely mountain scenery. With a trail network of over 200 km, the best way to explore the reserve is on foot, although guided game drives can be undertaken. The reserve has been stocked with wildebeest, red hartebeest, impala, blesbok and oribi. Also of interest is a guided walk to the Ngwenya Mine where iron ore was mined 43 000 years ago, making it the oldest mine in the world. Self-catering cabins are available, as are campsites.

From Malolotja the route heads south, joining the road to Mbabane at Motshane. Mbabane, the capital of Swaziland, is reached after 15 km. It is a bustling city with crowded streets and a variety of handicraft markets worth exploring. Crafts include colourful fabrics with batik-like patterns, grass mats and baskets, cowhide shields, bead necklaces and wood carvings.

On leaving Mbabane the road ascends the hills to the south before descending into the awe-inspiring Ezulwini Valley ('Place of Heaven'). Bounded in the east by the Mdimba Mountain, the valley extends for nearly 30 km to the southeast. The lush, densely vegetated valley is the tourist playground of Swaziland, with a casino, hotels, restaurants and handicraft stalls.

Approximately 9 km out of Mbabane you pass the village of Ludzidzini. Two of Swaziland's most important traditional ceremonies are held here – the *Umhlanga* or Reed Dance in August or September, and the *Ncwala* or First Fruits ceremony in late December or early January.

To the west of the valley lies the renowned Mlilwane Wildlife Sanctuary, established in 1964 by the Reilly family. Covering 4 500 ha, it is home to a variety of antelope, white rhino, hippo, crocodile, giraffe, Burchell's zebra, blue wildebeest and buffalo.

Visitors can go on self-guided or guided game drives, follow the trails over the hills and through the valleys, or they can go game viewing on horseback. Accommodation ranges from log cabins and thatched huts to beehive grass huts and a campsite. Mlilwane also has a restaurant.

Further down the Ezulwini Valley the road passes the Royal Village at Lobamba. Not to be missed is a visit to the Swaziland National Museum, with its fascinating displays depicting the history and culture of the Swazi people.

The route continues to Manzini and then heads south to Sidvokodvo and the junction with the Grand Valley road. After 7 km, turn left onto a back road to the village of Khubutha. The route now continues through grasslands dotted with grazing cattle, and further along it winds through deep valleys, streams and waving grasslands punctuated with an occasional kraal.

The next village, Sithobela, appears after a magnificent drive across the hills, and the road then passes through the lowveld to Maloma. From here it strikes west, passing through sugar cane plantations, cotton fields, thorn bush and kraals to Nsoko. The remainder of the route to Lavumisa is on tar.

JOZINI

From the Lavumisa/Golela border post the road skirts the 31 000-ha Pongolapoort Biosphere Reserve on the shores of the Pongolapoort Dam. On joining the N2, proceed for 28 km to the Jozini turnoff and turn left. As the road winds its way up the Ubombo Mountains you will have a spectacular view of the dam to the north. The waters of the Pongola River were harnassed in the 1960s when a 91-m-high wall was built across the 500-m-wide gorge between the Lebombo and Ubombo ranges.

The small settlement of Jozini has the atmosphere of a frontier town, with masses of informal traders selling their wares along the road winding through the town. Petrol is obtainable here. Jozini dates back to the late 1950s when it served as a construction village for the nearby dam.

From Jozini travel along the dam wall and head north across the Makatini Flats, a bush-covered plain straddling the Pongola River, to the Ndumo Game Reserve.

NDUMO GAME RESERVE

Pans, floodplains, fig forests, woodlands and grasslands merge in this 10 100-ha reserve to create one of South Africa's unique habitats. With a bird checklist of around 420 species it is regarded as one of the country's top birding spots. Species likely to be of interest to birders include the pygmy goose, Pel's fishing owl, Narina trogon, broadbilled roller and white-eared barbet.

Encompassing the Pongola and Usutu floodplains, Ndumo Game Reserve is characterized by several pans, the best known among them being Nyamithi, with its fever tree-lined banks, Banzi and Shokwe. The pans area is closed to private vehicles and Nyamithi and Banzi can be viewed only by joining a guided four-wheel drive tour conducted by the reserve authorities. Guided walks can be enjoyed along Shokwe, a horseshoe-shaped pan fringed by majestic sycamore figs.

About 300 hippo and 700 crocodiles (larger than 2 m) inhabit the pans and rivers, and the reserve has a large population of nyala. Other species to be seen include black and white rhino, giraffe, blue wildebeest, impala, red duiker and Burchell's zebra.

Accommodation in the Ndumo Hutted Camp is in thatched squaredavels, served by a communal kitchen (the meals are prepared by cooks) and hot and cold water ablutions. Situated at the western edge of Banzi Pan, the Ndumo Wilderness Camp offers luxury tented accommodation. The tariff is inclusive of all meals, as well as guided game-viewing drives in the Nyamithi and Banzi pans area.

Return to the tar road and then head east for 19 km to the signposted turnoff to the Tembe Elephant Park.

TEMBE ELEPHANT PARK

Situated a mere 5,5 km east of Ndumo, the main attraction of this 30 000-ha park is its 100-strong elephant population. They once belonged to a much larger population that used to migrate seasonally between southern Mozambique and the northern parts of Maputaland. However, as a result of the civil war in Mozambique, their numbers declined drastically, prompting the then Natal Bureau of Natural Resources to fence the northern boundary of the reserve in 1989.

Hippo, giraffe, Burchell's zebra, blue wildebeest, waterbuck, reedbuck, impala, nyala and both species of rhino occur here. Also to be seen is the rare suni, a species confined to sand forests. Birdlife is prolific and includes several sand forest species with a restricted distribution elsewhere in South Africa. Among these are the African broadbill, yellowspotted nicator, gorgeous bush shrike, Neergaardt's sunbird and pinkthroated twinspot.

Owing to the unpredictable and sometimes quite aggressive behaviour of the elephants, visitors are not permitted to explore the park without a game guard. Facilities include a small tented camp with a communal kitchen (meals are prepared by a cook) and hot and cold water ablutions, two hides and a self-guided trail surrounded by an elephant-proof fence.

From Tembe the route continues eastwards to Ngwanase and then for 12 km on gravel to Kosi Bay Nature Reserve. Otherwise you could follow the gravel road from Ngwanase for about 18 km to the border post to reach the delightful bay of Ponta do Ouro, just to the north of Kosi Mouth. After the border post the condition of the road deteriorates to thick sand, requiring a four-wheel drive vehicle or a vehicle with a high ground clearance.

PONTA DO OURO

After nearly two decades of neglect and decay, facilities at Ponta do Ouro (*see* page 135) have been renovated and refurbished and the resort is fast regaining the popularity it enjoyed prior to the outbreak of the country's civil war. The sheltered bay offers safe swimming, but most people are attracted by the snorkelling, scuba diving and fishing. Accommodation at the Motel de Mar consists of cabanas. The motel also has a restaurant.

KOSI BAY NATURE RESERVE

Kosi Bay, a string of pristine lakes and swamp forest situated along the Maputaland coast in the far northeastern corner of KwaZulu-Natal, is one of South Africa's unique spots. Comprising four lakes, the 18-km-long lake system is separated from the unspoilt beaches by forested dunes. The 10 961-ha reserve forms part of the Kosi Bay Coastal Forest Reserve and is popular among freshwater anglers. The mouth of the Kosi Bay estuary

Below: *At Kosi Bay the Tonga people still pursue their traditional way of fishing by using fish traps.*

71

offers wonderful opportunities for snorkelling and scuba diving. Accompanied by a trail guide, visitors can explore various areas of the nature reserve on foot. One of these trails is a full-day walk to Lake Amanzimyama, habitat of the uncommon raffia palm, where the rare palmnut vulture may be seen.

The rest camp on the banks of Lake Nhlange (Third Lake) has several campsites as well as three thatched lodges. You will also find a community-run campsite at the entrance gate to Kosi Mouth. However, the sandy track leading from the rest camp to Kosi Mouth is negotiable only by four-wheel drive vehicles. As the area is very sensitive, only a limited number of vehicles are permitted for day visits, so, if you want to spend some time here, the campsite at the entrance gate is ideal. Walks are conducted from the campsite to the traditional fish traps in Lake Makawulani (First Lake), an experience not to be missed.

From Kosi Bay, backtrack to Phelindaba and then head south to the signposted turnoff to Rocktail Bay. Follow the signposted roads to the entrance gate of the Kosi Bay Coastal Forest Reserve.

KOSI BAY COASTAL FOREST RESERVE

Covering nearly 33 000 ha, the Kosi Bay Forest Reserve incorporates Kosi Bay, the narrow 60-km-long coastal strip stretching from the Mozambican border to the Sodwana Bay National Park, and also Lake Sibaya.

Popular spots along the coast include Black Rock, Rocktail Bay and Lala Nek. The main attractions of this very remote and undeveloped area are its outstanding angling opportunities and its miles and miles of unspoilt beaches. Among the sought-after species are kingfish, barracuda, springer and shad. Rocktail Bay Reef and Lala Nek are two popular snorkelling spots.

Below: The coastline at Cape Vidal is flanked by high forested dunes that sweep down to miles of unspoilt beaches.

Accommodation in the reserve is limited to two options: a luxury lodge at Rocktail Bay and a campsite at Mabibi.

On leaving the reserve, travel west for 1,6 km and then turn south onto a road that skirts the eastern shores of Lake Sibaya.

LAKE SIBAYA

To the early inhabitants of the Maputaland coast this landlocked lake resembled a cattle pen, hence the name *isiBaya*. It is South Africa's largest inland freshwater lake, with an area of 7 750 ha.

Among fish species of interest to anglers are the Mozambique tilapia (the most abundant), the redbreast tilapia and the sharptooth catfish. Because of the poor quality of food in the water, the tilapia do not reach the same size as those that occur elsewhere. Private boats are not permitted, but boats with a coxswain can be hired. Birdlife is prolific and one of the best ways to see the diversity of waterbirds is to hire a boat from the camp and to explore the many bays and inlets. An excellent walk for birders is the 3,4-km Baya Camp Trail that meanders through coastal forests and umdoni woodlands to two hides overlooking small pans. Waterbirds here include the reed cormorant, greenbacked heron, whitefaced duck, pygmy goose and African fish eagle.

Rustic accommodation in reed-and-thatch huts is provided at Baya Camp on the southern shores of the lake. Amenities include a communal lounge and dining area (cooks are provided) and hot and cold water ablutions.

From Lake Sibaya the route continues to Mbazwana and then southwest on the Mhlosinga road to the signposted turnoff leading to the ranger's office in the Ozabeni segment of the Greater St Lucia Wetland Park.

OZABENI

Previously known as the Sodwana State Forest, the Ozabeni section of the Greater St Lucia Wetland Park consists of almost

48 000 ha of grasslands, palmveld, fig forests, papyrus swamps and seasonal pans. It is one of the least known parts of the park and access is restricted to the area west of the Mbazwana River. Owing to the sandy terrain, the tracks are negotiable only by four-wheel drive vehicles. Although there are no designated hiking trails, the more adventurous visitor can also arrange to explore the area on foot. Another way of discovering this impressive wilderness and its rich variety of birdlife is to join a canoeing trip conducted on the pans by Ntini Safaris.

The pans and swamps are home to a population of over 100 hippo and large numbers of crocodiles. Impala, reedbuck, nyala, bushbuck, kudu, waterbuck, Burchell's zebra, oribi and red duiker have been reintroduced, while leopard and hyena also occur. Ozabeni is a rewarding birding destination and in excess of 360 species have been recorded here to date. Birdlife includes the white pelican, Goliath and rufousbellied herons, the lesser jacana, crowned crane, longtoed plover, black coucal, broadbilled roller and green twinspot.

Facilities in this section of the park are limited to a basic campsite alongside the Manzimbomu River.

From Ozabeni the route leads in a southwesterly direction, passing the 15 000-ha Phinda Resource Reserve, to Mhlosinga. The route then heads north along the old Hluhluwe road to the signposted turnoff to the Mkuzi Game Reserve.

MKUZI GAME RESERVE

Mkuzi became an integral part of the Greater St Lucia Wetland Park when the farmland separating it from Ozabeni was acquired in the early 1990s. Covering 36 000 ha of savanna, sand forest,

Above: *At Kosi Bay on the Maputaland coast, a string of pristine lakes has created a unique wetland system, one of the most remarkable in South Africa.*

thickets, floodplains, grasslands and pans, it is a firm favourite with many nature-lovers. It offers superb game viewing and among the species to be seen are black and white rhinos, blue wildebeest, giraffe, Burchell's zebra, impala, kudu and reedbuck. The reserve has a large population of common duiker, while suni can sometimes be found in the sand forest.

Visitors can follow the road network in search of game, or they can spend time at one of the four game-viewing hides. The two viewing platforms overlooking the Nsumu Pan provide an excellent opportunity to observe the hippos and crocodiles, and also the birdlife of the pan. A number of delightful picnic spots can be found throughout the reserve.

One of the highlights of a visit to Mkuzi is the Fig Forest Walk in the southeastern section of the park. It is an easy 3-km self-guided walk through an impressive forest of sycamore figs and it offers good opportunities for birding. Guided early morning game-viewing and birding walks are also available. On the guided night drives visitors can make use of a powerful spotlight to search for nocturnal animals such as porcupine, hyena and other nocturnal predators.

Accommodation ranges from bungalows and a tented camp at Mantuma to bush lodges and a campsite near the entrance gate.

From the Mkuzi Game Reserve the route continues to the N2 and then leads south to the signposted turnoff at Hluhluwe village, continuing to Memorial Gate.

Above: One of the main attractions of the Hluhluwe-Umfolozi Park is the large number of white rhino.
Left: Muntulu Bush Lodge accommodates visitors in luxury in the wilds of the Hluhluwe-Umfolozi Park.
Opposite: The Hluhluwe-Umfolozi Park in Zululand is home to about 2 000 Burchell's zebra.
Following pages: The Ezulwini Valley, south of Mbabane, is a mosaic of grasslands, plantations and forests.

HLUHLUWE-UMFOLOZI PARK

Set aside for conservation in 1895, this is the oldest protected area in Africa. Previously two separate reserves, Hluhluwe-Umfolozi covers 96 000 ha of rolling hills and valleys in central Zululand, an area interwoven with the history of the Zulu nation.

The park is renowned for its abundance of game, including the Big Five (lion, leopard, elephant, rhino and buffalo). The Umfolozi section in the south is closely linked to the successful efforts in the 1960s to save the white rhino from extinction. The black rhino and buffalo populations here are healthy, and hippo, giraffe and several antelope species also occur.

A network of roads criss-crosses the park, some forming part of three interpretative drives. Other activities include short, self-guided walks, guided game-viewing walks, wilderness trails and night drives. Hides at waterholes provide an opportunity to see game at close quarters, especially during the dry winter. Visitors can alight from their vehicles at a number of picnic spots.

A wide range of accommodation is available. Hilltop in the Hluhluwe section of the park offers modern thatched bungalows and rondavels with communal kitchen and ablution facilities, and Mtwazi Lodge provides the ultimate in luxury. Accommodation in the Umfolozi section is available at Masinda, quite a small camp, or at Mpila Camp. The park's three bush lodges and three bush camps offer a true wilderness experience.

Leave Umfolozi through Cengeni Gate, head for Ulundi (*see* Zululand, page 62) and continue to Vryheid. The route returns to Johannesburg via Piet Retief, Ermelo and Bethal.

Southern Kalahari

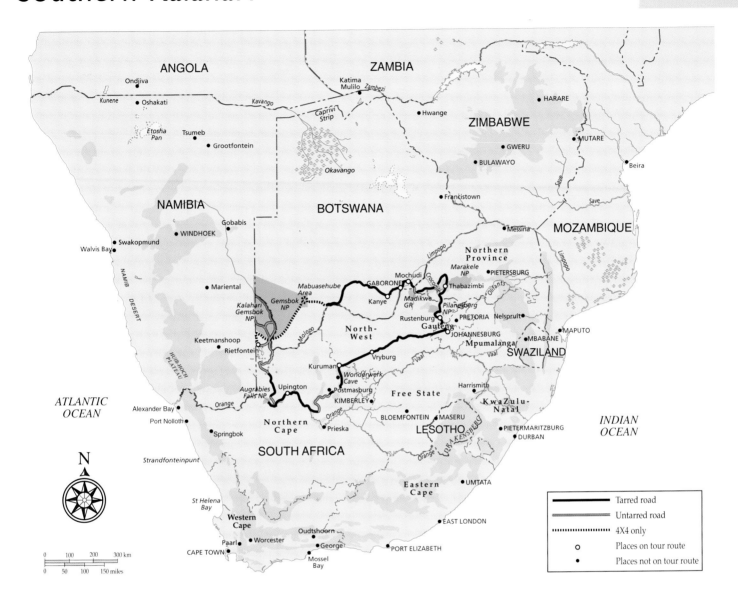

6

This 4 500-km tour explores the vast, desolate expanses of the southern Kalahari in the Northern Cape Province and Botswana. As the area is very remote, a party of at least two four-wheel drive vehicles, which must be equipped for emergencies, is essential. The tour takes about three weeks to complete and the sandy terrain will test driving skills to the limit – the more challenging sections are best left to those with experience of driving in sand.

KURUMAN

From Johannesburg, head west for 420 km on the N14 to Vryburg, where you join the Namakwari Route, a tourist route linking the Kalahari and Namaqualand. You will reach Kuruman, centre of agriculture and mining in the Kalahari, after 140 km.

Opposite: *The Kalahari Gemsbok National Park in the Northern Cape is named after the hardy gemsbok.*

With its leafy palm trees, willows and lush vegetation in an otherwise barren landscape, Kuruman is known as the 'Oasis of the Kalahari'. The town developed around a spring which was named *Gasegonyane* ('little water calabash') by the early Tswana inhabitants. Crystal-clear water flows to the surface at a rate of 20 to 30 million litres a day and the spring is said to be the most prodigious in the southern hemisphere.

Worth visiting is the Kalahari Raptor Rehabilitation Centre, where injured raptors are treated and returned to the wild. Of historic interest is the Moffat Mission, established in 1820 by the Scottish missionary Robert Moffat. The complex comprises several relics from the early mission days, including the stone church built by Moffat in 1836. Also to be seen here is the tree under which the missionary and explorer, David Livingstone, proposed marriage to Mary Moffat. The Moffat homestead and the historic wagon house are also part of the complex.

Above: The Augrabies Falls are one of the best examples of a cataract-type waterfall in the world. The Main Falls plunge 56 m into a gorge carved into granite by the river.

WONDERWERK CAVE

This fascinating cave is situated on the farm Wonderwerk, 42 km south of Kuruman on the Daniëlskuil road. South Africa's oldest known mobile art – engravings on stone slabs – was discovered in the cave and dated to about 10 000 years ago. Other artefacts excavated include stone implements, decorated ostrich eggshells and animal bones. Adorning the walls of the cave are monochrome rock paintings. Also of interest are a large stalagmite near the entrance of the cave, as well as stalactites which are active after good rains. A nearby exhibition centre houses displays depicting the geology and archaeology of the area.

Proceed from the Wonderwerk Cave towards Daniëlskuil and Postmasburg. From here the route follows the back roads via Bermolli and the Bergenaarspad Pass over the Langberg to the Witsand Nature Reserve.

WITSAND NATURE RESERVE

With the Langberg forming a striking backdrop to the west, the white sand dunes of Witsand provide a sharp contrast to the surrounding sea of red dunes. Adding to the beauty of this unique landscape are pools of crystal-clear water seeping to the surface from vast subterranean reservoirs. Another attraction is Brulsand, meaning 'roaring sands', situated near the southern edge of Witsand – the dunes roar with a reverberating sound when the dry sand is disturbed. Tubes of fused silica are common here. Known as fulgurites, these tubes are formed when lightning strikes the ground; their abundance in the area has been ascribed to the high elevation of the dunes.

The route then continues to the southwest, along back roads and over the Padkloof Pass, to the Kimberley/Upington road and then on to Upington.

UPINGTON

Upington is an important centre for the processing of sultanas, grapes, and other produce cultivated on the fertile banks of the Orange River, and wine. Places of interest include the Palm Tree Avenue on Die Eiland (at over 1 km it is the longest such avenue in the southern hemisphere), the South African Dried Fruit Cooperative (the second largest in the world) and the Orange River Wine Cooperative (also the second largest in the world).

AUGRABIES FALLS NATIONAL PARK

Situated some 120 km west of Upington, this national park encompasses one of South Africa's greatest natural wonders – the spectacular Augrabies Falls. Above the falls, the river fans out and accelerates rapidly down a series of cataracts before plunging thunderously into a deep gorge. The Main Falls are 56 m high, but when the river is in flood a multitude of waterfalls tumble noisily into the 18-km-long gorge. Viewpoints with safety rails along the edge of the gorge provide breathtaking views of the falls. Be very careful, however, where there are no safety railings – Augrabies has claimed many lives.

Visitors to the national park can go on scenic drives, undertake short walks, or simply enjoy the beauty, peace and tranquillity of their surroundings. The more energetic can tackle the three-day Klipspringer Hiking Trail, and for the truly adventurous the Augrabies Three-In-One Adventure – a combination of canoeing, hiking and mountain biking – is a must. Visitors can also join the Black Rhino Adventure, a guided four-wheel drive excursion, in search of the black rhinos living in the northern section of the park.

From Augrabies, the route continues through Vrouenspan, Koopan-Suid and Inkbospan to the Kalahari Molopo Lodge, 60 km south of the Kalahari Gemsbok National Park.

KALAHARI 4x4 TRAIL

Starting at the Kalahari Molopo Lodge, this guided 250-km circular route traverses the dunelands of the Mier area, sandwiched between the Kalahari Gemsbok National Park and Namibia. The first 100 km is on proclaimed gravel roads, but from Rietfontein the trail passes into the undulating Kalahari dunes. This section of the trail includes some very exciting dune driving, and drivers receive the necessary instruction and practice before negotiating the dunes.

The amenities at the reed-and-thatch overnight stop at Polai include beds, shower, flush toilet and a braai area. The return leg of the trail follows the boundary fence of the Kalahari Gemsbok National Park to Twee Rivieren, the park's main rest camp. Groups must consist of a minimum of three vehicles, while single-vehicle parties can join larger groups.

KALAHARI GEMSBOK NATIONAL PARK

Dominating the scenic splendour of this 959 000-ha park are the wonderful red dunes of the Kalahari. The park is a sanctuary to herds of gemsbok, springbok, red hartebeest, eland and blue wildebeest. It is also home to the famed blond-maned Kalahari lions and a healthy population of brown hyena, while spotted hyena, leopard and cheetah also occur. Several giraffe were reintroduced into the park in 1990, 87 years after the last one was shot in the area. Since no fence exists between the Kalahari Gemsbok National Park and the adjacent Gemsbok National Park in Botswana, the animals are able to migrate freely between the two national parks.

After the first summer rains large herds of springbok are attracted to the green flush of grass in the river beds, while gemsbok, blue wildebeest and red hartebeest are found in the river beds at the end of the rainy season. Eland are generally confined to the central area of the park, but they move about constantly in search of grazing.

Forty of South Africa's 67 raptors and seven species of owls have been recorded in the Kalahari region, and the Kalahari Gemsbok National Park is one of the best places to see these birds. Viewing is most rewarding between February and April, especially after good rains. Among the species to be seen in the park are the bateleur, the rednecked falcon, blackbreasted snake eagle, martial eagle and pygmy falcon.

Owing to the dune landscape, the road network of the park is largely limited to the dry beds of the Auob and Nossob rivers. There are, however, two connecting routes between the rivers. All roads are well-maintained and are negotiable by sedan car.

Accommodation is available at Twee Rivieren (the park's main rest camp, situated at the southern entrance), Mata Mata (alongside the border with Namibia), and Nossob (70 km north of Twee Rivieren). A number of unfenced picnic sites with toilet facilities are scattered throughout the park.

From Twee Rivieren, backtrack to the border post at Bokspits, and after completing border formalities travel north to the game scout camp (which is also known as Twee Rivieren) in Botswana's Gemsbok National Park.

GEMSBOK NATIONAL PARK

With its typical Kalahari scenery and wildlife, one of the main attractions of this park is its wilderness atmosphere. As a result of the sparse and erratic rainfall, the game and the predators are highly mobile, and the Kalahari is renowned for its mass migration of antelope. During the rainy season large herds of antelope congregate in the Nossob River bed to feed on the nutritious grass. They also frequent the pans in the dunes, dispersing into the dunes during winter.

The Gemsbok National Park was closed to the public until the mid-1990s and, although it is slowly being opened up, it is still important to obtain the necessary permits prior to entering the park. Plans are afoot to develop a circular 4x4 trail, but in the meantime visitors are permitted to travel to Mabuasehube along the park boundary road. This road is not only extremely sandy, but also quite remote and it is therefore essential to discuss the details of your trip with the game scouts at Twee Rivieren (Botswana). They will then radio the group's expected time of arrival at Mabuasehube to the game scout camp there.

Take special care when driving through long grass: vehicles have actually been set alight by grass caught up by the protection plate. Since no designated campsites exist along the way, visitors should be very careful not to cause veld fires when camping out and should also be on the alert for predators.

MABUASEHUBE

Aptly known in the Kgalagadi tongue as 'Place of Red Earth', Mabuasehube adjoins the Gemsbok National Park to the east and it now forms an integral part of the park. Six large clay pans fringed by dunes of up to 30 m high, as well as a series of smaller pans separated by small dunes, form the focal point of this reserve. Each pan has its own attractions: Bosobogolo, the southernmost pan, is usually covered with short grass, while Mabuasehube has a barren clay floor.

Game viewing depends on local rainfall as the herds of game migrate freely throughout this 1,8-million-ha sanctuary in search of grazing. Typical Kalahari game species include eland, springbok, gemsbok, blue wildebeest and red hartebeest. The summer months generally offer the most rewarding game viewing. In addition to the usual Kalahari species, you will probably be able to see Cape fox, aardwolf and brown hyena at Mabuasehube, while lion, leopard and wild dog also occur there.

Below: The bat-eared fox is one of three jackal species occurring in the Kalahari Gemsbok National Park.

Although camping is permitted at the Mpayathulwa, Khiding, Mabuasehube and Lesholoago pans, visitors should come well prepared as no facilities whatsoever are available there.

From Mpayathulwa Pan the route heads east for about 96 km. After crossing Goa Pan, you will reach a small village, after which the track swings southeast for about 27 km where it joins the Tshabong/Werda tar road. Continue via Sekoma, Jwaneng and Kanye to Lobatse and then head north to Mochudi (*see* page 90). Leave Botswana through the Sikwane/Derdepoort border post and proceed to the Madikwe Game Reserve.

MADIKWE GAME RESERVE

Madikwe has a wonderful diversity of interesting landscapes and vegetation, with scenery ranging from quartzite hills and bushveld to *inselberge* (island mountains) and savanna plains. The 75 000-ha game reserve is bounded in the south by the Dwarsberg, while the Marico River forms a natural boundary in the east. In the north it shares a common boundary with Botswana for approximately 70 km.

Within the past 15 or so years, the area has changed from overgrazed farmland to one of Southern Africa's prime eco-tourism destinations. In one of the largest wildlife translocation projects in Africa, Operation Phoenix, some 10 000 animals of 27 species were reintroduced into the reserve.

Madikwe is home to the Big Five and is a sanctuary to the largest elephant population outside the Kruger National Park. The reserve is situated in a transition area, and game from the arid west as well as typical Lowveld species are found here. Among the antelope are springbok, impala, gemsbok, tsessebe, eland, waterbuck, blue wildebeest and common reedbuck. Other inhabitants of Madikwe are Burchell's zebra, hippo, giraffe, wild dog, cheetah and spotted hyena.

The reserve is aimed at the more exclusive end of the market and lodges cater for guests on a fully-inclusive basis. Activities include early morning and late afternoon or night game-viewing drives, guided walks and delectable bush braais.

From Madikwe, travel via Kaya se Put and Dwaalboom to Thabazimbi, a mining town and centre for the surrounding cattle-farming district, and on to the Marakele National Park.

MARAKELE NATIONAL PARK

Covering 15 000 square kilometres, the Waterberg comprises several conservation areas, among them the Marakele National Park at the western end of the range. Sheer cliffs, sandstone buttresses, deep gorges, sparkling streams and grassy plains combine here to create breathtaking scenery.

Four of the Big Five already occur in the park and lions will be introduced once antelope have increased to such an extent that they can sustain these predators. In addition to elephant, rhino, buffalo and leopard, the park also has hippo, giraffe, Burchell's zebra, eland, kudu, red hartebeest, roan, sable and tsessebe.

Although the core of the park was established in 1988, it received national park status only in 1994 and is still being developed. At present the only facility is a tented camp that is accessible by four-wheel drive vehicle. Directions to the camp are provided when you make reservations.

PILANESBERG NATIONAL PARK

From Thabazimbi travel south via Northam and Mogwase to Pilanesberg National Park, a Big Five game park situated in an extinct volcano. Sanctuary to the world's third largest population of white rhino, this is a good place to see this species. Roaming the bushveld are gemsbok, springbok, blue wildebeest, impala, waterbuck, kudu, giraffe and Burchell's zebra, while hippo inhabit Mankwe Lake. Birdlife is prolific and the 'walk-in' aviary at the Manyane complex and the nearby Mothata vulture restaurant are worth a visit. You will find a number of hides, viewpoints and picnic spots throughout the park. Accommodation options range from tented camps and campsites to three luxury lodges and the glitzy Sun City and Lost City on the park's southern boundary.

From Pilanesberg it is a comfortable 90-minute drive back to Johannesburg via Rustenburg and the Hartbeespoort Dam.

Opposite: *The Kalahari Gemsbok National Park is home to about 100 cheetah. Their main species of prey is springbok.*

Above: *Large areas of the Waterberg in the Northern Province have been set aside for conservation and the area is fast becoming a prime ecotourism destination.*

Right: *Twee Rivieren Rest Camp in the Kalahari Gemsbok National Park lies at the junction of the Auob and Nossob rivers, hence its name.*

Left: *Camel thorn trees straining under the weight of sociable weavers' nests are a familiar sight in the Kalahari.*

Top: *The bateleur, a magnificent bird in flight, is frequently seen in the Kalahari Gemsbok National Park.*

Above: *The gemsbok cucumber is a favoured food of the gemsbok and is generally their only source of sustenance during droughts.*

Following pages: *A rainbow holds out hope of rain in the Kalahari Gemsbok National Park, which is often ravaged by years and years of drought.*

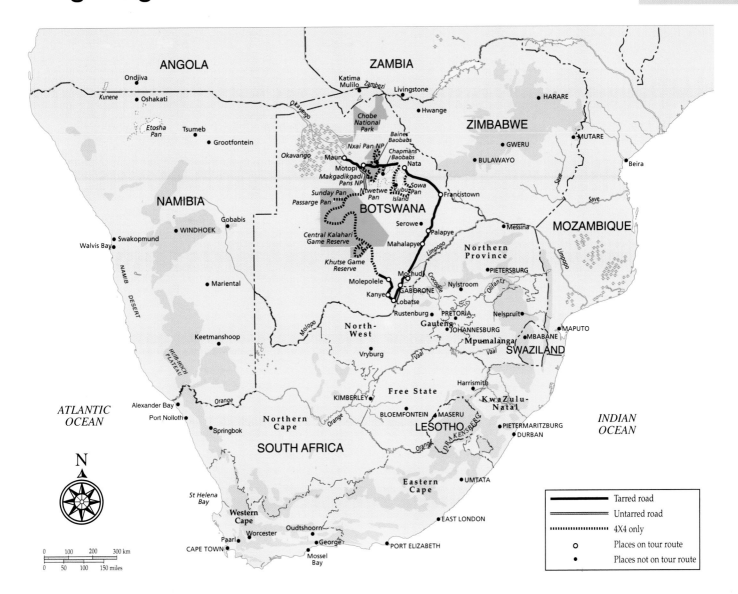

Few places in Africa are as remote and wild as the vast expanses of Botswana's Makgadikgadi Pans and Central Kalahari. In addition to game viewing, visitors can enjoy the remarkable scenery and the solitude. Cultural sites along the route provide an insight into the way of life of the Tswana and San people.

This tour requires thorough preparation, and parties should consist of at least two four-wheel drive vehicles, equipped with the necessary spares for emergency repairs. During summer you should take particular care to prevent grass seeds from blocking the radiator and grass from accumulating under the protection plate below the vehicle. Distances are vast and you will have to take along sufficient fuel – the longest stretch between filling stations is 1 200 km. The tour takes three weeks to complete.

Opposite: *The thick, loose sand in Botswana's Central Kalahari necessitates the constant use of four-wheel drive.*

You can combine this 4 500-km tour with Tour 8 (*see* page 99), which covers northern Botswana – circling the Okavango Delta and taking in Chobe National Park and Moremi Game Reserve.

GABORONE

In just over 30 years Gaborone, the capital of Botswana, has grown from a village of 6 000 people to a city with over 250 000 people. It is Africa's fastest-growing urban area. The modern glass and concrete high-rise buildings that dominate the inner city contrast sharply with the sprawling self-help housing areas on the outskirts of the city.

Visitors will find several places of interest in and around Gaborone, among them the National Museum with its excellent displays depicting the people and fauna of Botswana. You could also pay a visit to the Gaborone Game Reserve, which is situated on the northeastern outskirts of the city. Covering about 550 ha of woodlands, bushveld, riverine vegetation and reedbeds, the reserve has been stocked with eland, kudu, gemsbok, impala, blue wildebeest and Burchell's zebra.

MOCHUDI

Approximately 34 km north of Gaborone a signpost points the way to Mochudi, 'capital' of the Bakgatla tribe. Built around Phuthadikobo Hill, the historical core of Mochudi has some fine examples of traditional Bakgatla houses and granaries. The buildings are centered around the *kgotla* (courtyard) where tribal meetings and court sessions are held.

From the *kgotla* a footpath takes you to the Phuthadikobo Museum. Housed in the Mochudi National School, Botswana's first secondary school, the museum contains an excellent display of early photographs of the settlement as well as an ethnographic collection. Part of the school is occupied by a silkscreen workshop, renowned for its traditional and modern designs. Another interesting feature of the village is that the two southernmost baobabs in Botswana grow here.

A few kilometres north of Mochudi an inconspicuous track turns off to the right and after about 500 m reaches Matsieng – a hole in a sheet of rock. Surrounding the rock are a number of engravings of animal spoor and also one of a human footprint. The Batswana people believe that the very first human beings and animals emerged from this hole.

NATA

Further north, the route passes through the towns of Mahalapye and Palapye to reach Botswana's second largest town, Francistown. From here it strikes northwest, skirting the mopane and

Below: Botswana's landscape is dotted with numerous pans that become inundated after the summer rains, bringing relief to people and animals alike.

acacia woodlands, to reach Nata, a small settlement at the junction of the western road leading to Maun and the northern one to Kazungula, Chobe National Park and Victoria Falls.

Nata is an ideal stopover and a convenient base for exploring the Nata Bird Sanctuary at the northeastern end of Sowa Pan. The core of the 31 000-ha sanctuary is the Nata River delta which attracts up to 250 000 flamingoes during the dry winter months. Large numbers of pelicans, waterfowl and waders also congregate around the delta.

The recommended route to Makgadikgadi Pans and Kubu Island goes south via the villages of Mosu and Mmatshumo.

MAKGADIKGADI PANS

Covering approximately 1 200 000 ha, Makgadikgadi consists of two main pans – Sowa in the east and the much larger Ntwetwe in the west – as well as a series of smaller pans. These are a relic of an enormous inland lake, larger than Lake Victoria, which covered much of northern Botswana half a million years ago. Fringing the pans are stately palm trees and extensive grasslands.

Stretching for more than 100 km from north to south, the whitish-grey surface of Sowa Pan fades away into the distance. To the west lies Ntwetwe Pan, separated from Sowa by a narrow tongue of grassland. Dust devils dance across the floor of the pan, while shimmering mirages play havoc with the imagination. Contributing to Makgadikgadi's unique atmosphere is the total silence. In the late afternoon, the harsh surface of the pans is transformed into magical rosy pink tones.

One of the chief attractions of the Makgadikgadi area is Kubu Island, an isolated granite outcrop studded with stunted baobab trees. Also worth seeing are Green's Baobab and Chapman's Baobabs, two well-known landmarks used by traders and travellers during the mid-1800s. These particular baobabs are situated south of the settlement of Gweta, where you will find a lodge and a filling station.

A journey across the pans should not be taken lightly and parties should consist of at least two vehicles equipped with recovery equipment. The surface of the pans can be extremely deceptive – it appears solid, but below the thin crust is a treacherous quagmire of mud. Between June and September is generally the safest time to travel here, but this period can be extended by a month each way during years of low rainfall.

Getting bogged down is not the only obstacle with which travellers might have to cope. Being caught in a sandstorm can be a frightening experience and the best advice in this situation is to stay put until the storm has abated.

MAKGADIKGADI PANS NATIONAL PARK

This scenic park incorporates the northwestern corner of Ntwetwe Pan and is a lovely mosaic of open grasslands and shimmering pans, fringed by groves of tall palm trees. Lush riverine forests grow along the Boteti River, which forms the park's western boundary.

During the winter months vast herds of Burchell's zebra and blue wildebeest are attracted to the grasslands in the east of the park. As the water in the pans dries up, they migrate to the Boteti River. Other game species to be seen here include springbok, gemsbok, red hartebeest, giraffe, lion and cheetah.

Camping areas have been designated at Njuca Hills and at Khumaga on the banks of the Boteti River.

NXAI PAN NATIONAL PARK

Adjoining the Makgadikgadi Pans National Park to the north is Nxai Pan National Park. The turnoff is 24 km west of the main entry point to the Makgadikgadi Pans National Park.

The road to the north traverses the Kanyu Flats, an extensive grassland studded with a number of small pans as well as a large, sterile pan – Kudiakam. Baines' Baobabs, on the eastern edge of Kudiakam, are a popular attraction. These trees were named after the explorer Thomas Baines, who painted them in 1862, during his journey from Namibia to Victoria Falls.

Centered around a 40-square-kilometre grass-covered pan interspersed with acacia tree islands, Nxai Pan National Park supports large herds of blue wildebeest, Burchell's zebra and gemsbok between December and April. The park is renowned for its large giraffe population and herds of up to 50 animals are not at all uncommon. Springbok, impala, kudu, red hartebeest, spotted and brown hyaenas, and cheetah also occur here.

To the northeast of Nxai Pan lies the smaller Kgama-Kgama Pan which, like its sister pans Nxai and Kudiakam, once formed part of a vast inland lake.

South Camp, on the southern edge of Nxai Pan, is a popular campsite as it offers good shade and has the added attraction of a nearby lookout and hide. In its setting of mopane veld, North Camp does not overlook the pan and has little shade.

From the park, backtrack to the main road and then continue for about 140 km to Maun, a sprawling town on the banks of the Thamalakane River.

Above: *Baines' Baobabs, situated on the eastern edge of Kudiakam Pan, are a very well-known landmark in the Nxai Pan National Park.*

MAUN

As recently as 20 years ago Maun (*see also* page 99) had the image of a Wild West frontier town, but the completion of the tar road from Nata has changed all this. Modern shopping complexes with speciality shops have replaced the old trading stores, and the dusty streets have given way to tar roads and paved sidewalks. The only landmarks that have remained are the legendary Riley's Hotel and Riley's Garage. Several lodges are situated in and around the town.

The Maun Game Reserve, located on the eastern banks of the Thamalakane River, serves as an educational park. The 300-ha reserve incorporates the reed beds after which Maun ('Place of Reeds') has been named. Animals to be seen here include giraffe, Burchell's zebra, kudu, red lechwe, impala and warthog.

Maun is the gateway to the Okavango Delta, and a *mokoro* (dugout canoe) trip in the Delta is an unforgettable experience. While lodges in the Delta cater for upmarket visitors, Oddball's Palm Island Camping Lodge offers campsites and reasonably priced *mokoro* trips. After a 20-minute flight to the island, guests set off in *mekoro* to explore the fascinating waterways.

CENTRAL KALAHARI GAME RESERVE

Approaching from the north, the best way to reach this game reserve is by travelling from Maun via Motopi village, from where a graded road winds along the Boteti River to Rakops. Take in sufficient fuel here to cover the journey of at least 1 200 km to the next refuelling stop, Molepolele.

From Rakops the route continues in a southwesterly direction to reach the park gate after 49 km and the game scout camp after another 9 km. The tracks in the north of the Central Kalahari Game Reserve are generally hard, but during the rainy season vehicles can get bogged down on the clay surfaces and in the pans. In the south, thick loose sand has to be negotiated, especially in the section between Xade and Khankhe Pan.

Covering about 5 280 000 ha of open woodland, sandveld and scrub, the Central Kalahari Game Reserve is the second largest conservation area in the world, surpassed in size only by the Selous Game Reserve in southern Tanzania. Contrary to what one might expect, the scenery is generally flat and surprisingly well vegetated. Sand dunes and small pans do occur, but mainly in the north of the reserve.

The main attractions of the Central Kalahari are undoubtedly its wilderness atmosphere, wide open spaces, solitude and also its seasonal concentrations of game. The best time for game viewing is during the summer months, when large herds of gemsbok, springbok and blue wildebeest congregrate in the north of the reserve. Also to be seen are red hartebeest, kudu and giraffe. Following the tracks of the migratory herds are the predators – lion, hyena and cheetah.

One of the most popular areas in the reserve is Deception Pan, situated at the northeastern edge of the 80-km-long Deception Valley. The singular beauty of the area was popularized in the mid-1980s by husband-and-wife team Mark and Delia Owens in their book *Cry of the Kalahari*. Other places of interest in the reserve include Piper's, Passarge and Sunday pans.

The park was originally proclaimed as a reserve for the San and Bakgalakgadi hunter-gatherers who have lived here for centuries. As a result, public access was severely restricted until the early 1990s and special permission was needed to visit the reserve. In the south are several settlements, the largest being at Xade, which boasts a clinic, a school and a small shop. A visit to the San settlement at Molapo with its traditional grass huts will prove to be an interesting experience.

KHUTSE GAME RESERVE

Immediately to the south of the Central Kalahari Game Reserve is Khutse Game Reserve. Here, rolling grasslands, pans and fossil dunes combine to form a dramatically beautiful landscape.

In the northeastern corner of the reserve lies a series of pans in a fossil river, relics of a wetter period thousands of years ago. The pans are called 'Place where you can kneel down to drink'.

You will not generally encounter large herds of antelope, but, when the pans do hold water, game sometimes congregates there. Species most likely to be seen are gemsbok, springbok, blue wildebeest, red hartebeest, kudu and eland. Lion, cheetah, wild dog and both species of hyena also occur.

The reserve has several campsites, all of which are located on the edge of the pans, except those near Molose waterhole.

MOLEPOLELE

From Khutse the route heads in a southeasterly direction along a track with deep sand to Letlhakeng, where it joins a tar road. It then continues to Molepolele, a large traditional village and the 'capital' of the Kwena tribe. It is one of only two modern villages where you can see the stone walls that were traditionally built by the Tswana to separate family enclosures. About 10 km to the west of the village lies Dithejwane Hill, where what remains of the old Kwena capital, Dithubaruba, can be seen.

MOKOLODI NATURE RESERVE

Instead of going directly from Molepolele to Gaborone, travel via Thamaga and Kanye to Lobatse and then head north from here to the village of Otse. Punctuating the woodlands and sandveld surrounding Otse are several sandstone hills. A short way to the southeast of the village lies the Mannyelanong Vulture Sanctuary, established in 1985 to provide protection for the only remaining breeding colony of the Cape vulture in Botswana. The population currently stands at about 90 pairs.

A visit to Mokolodi Nature Reserve 14 km south of Gaborone will be well worth your while. Covering approximately 3 000 ha, the reserve has been stocked with mountain reedbuck, kudu, eland, Burchell's zebra, giraffe, white rhino and hippo.

Mokolodi is also a sanctuary for young orphaned elephants, and visitors can go for walks with the elephants to explore the reserve. Some other activities offered at Mokolodi include rhino tracking, guided walks and game-viewing drives.

The reserve has several self-catering chalets, a thatched *à la carte* restaurant and a bar.

Opposite: An ingenious road sign near Rakops, the closest village to the northern gate of the Central Kalahari Game Reserve.

Above: The lions of the Kalahari seem to have adapted to living in their harsh desert environment.

Right: The Central Kalahari Game Reserve is characterized by endless expanses of thornveld and grassland that seem to merge with the horizon.

Top: *Travellers must keep an eye out for domestic stock on Botswana's roads. These animals roam free, even far off the highways.*

Above: *Maun, on the banks of the Thamalakane River, is the gateway to the Okavango Delta, a wonderworld of reed-lined channels, papyrus swamps, oxbow lakes and waterways.*

Right: *Camping in the vastness of the Central Kalahari Game Reserve, Africa's second largest conservation area.*

Following pages: *Springbok and gemsbok are the two most common antelope species to be seen in the Nxai Pan National Park.*

Okavango Delta, Chobe and Moremi

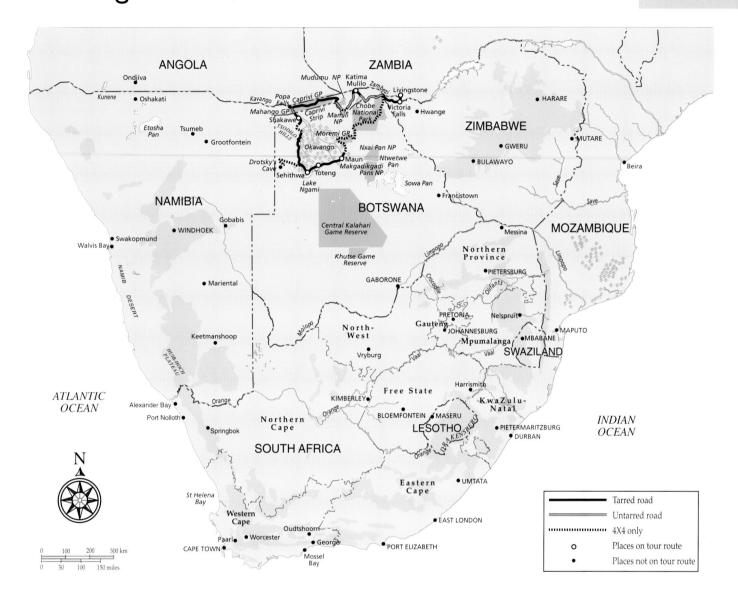

8

This tour explores one of the world's greatest natural wonders, the Okavango Delta. It includes the remote Drotsky's Caves and Tsodilo Hills and some of Namibia's lesser-known parks, and ends after three to four weeks with two of Africa's finest game parks – Chobe and Moremi. Although much of the 2 900-km route has been tarred, a four-wheel drive vehicle is essential and the route is not recommended for single-vehicle parties.

THE OKAVANGO DELTA
Situated on the edge of the Okavango Delta, the town of Maun (*see also* page 91) is the springboard for trips into the Okavango, a 1 600 000-ha wilderness of meandering channels, oxbow lakes, floodplains, reedbeds and tree-covered islands.

Opposite: *One of the best ways of exploring the Okavango Delta is by* mokoro *(dugout canoe).*

Several luxury lodges are situated in the permanently flooded delta, all offering guided walks, *mokoro* (dugout canoe), boat and fishing trips, while lodges in the seasonally inundated delta also conduct guided game-viewing trips.

Camping is possible at Gunn's Camp and Oddball's Palm Island Camping Lodge, from where you can take guided *mokoro* trips into the Delta. Both camps are accessible by air from Maun. You can spend days gliding along the narrow, water lily-carpeted channels in traditional canoes, punted expertly by a poler. During the heat of the day the shady riverine forests provide a welcome respite from the sun, and camping at night is in the open on one of the many small islands along the Boro River.

With over 400 birds recorded in the Okavango Delta to date, a canoe trip is one of the best ways to see some of the area's specials – slaty egret, wattled crane, coppertailed coucal, Pel's fishing owl, greater swamp warbler and swamp boubou.

Top: This panel of rock paintings at the Tsodilo Hills was named after Sir Lourens van der Post.
Above: The Tsodilo Hills, Botswana's most significant rock art site, is a national monument.

LAKE NGAMI

From Maun, head southwest on the Sehithwa road, continuing past the settlement of Toteng. Keep an eye out for a turnoff signposted 'Fishing Camp' about 4 km before you reach the village of Sehithwa. This road provides the easiest access to the lake shore, but a detour is only worthwhile if there is water.

Once part of an enormous lake, natural changes have reduced Ngami to an ephemeral lake, often dry for years at a time. During exceptional floods, however, an area of up to about 250 square kilometres becomes inundated. Tens of thousands of greater and lesser flamingoes, pelicans and storks, as well as millions of waterfowl, are then attracted to the lake. Local fishermen also exploit the rich fish resource, hence the signpost to the Fishing Camp.

The area is inhabited by the descendants of the Herero people who fled from Namibia to Botswana in 1904 to escape from the repression of the German colonial administration. In 1994 many of the Botswana Hereros returned to Namibia, but some of the older people elected to stay, and Herero ladies in their Victorian-style dresses are a common sight.

DROTSKY'S CAVES

From Sehithwa, take the Shakawe road for 11 km beyond the village of Tsao to the turnoff to Drostky's Caves. The track is initially hard, but once you reach the dunes the going becomes more difficult. The turnoff to the caves is signposted 147 km from the Shakawe road and the caves are 28 km further.

Close to Botswana's border with Namibia, these magnificent caverns extend for 500 m into the dolomitic Gcwihaba Hills. They were formed millions of years ago when water percolated along fractures into the rock, dissolving the dolomite.

Since the caves are totally undeveloped, it is essential to have a strong torch, spare batteries and emergency lighting. Once inside the dark caverns, a wonderworld of stalactites, stalagmites and flowstone unfolds in the light of a torch.

A number of informal campsites can be found near the two entrances to the caves, but no water is available. Also worth visiting is the nearby San village of Ncwama, as well as Xaixai and the Aha Hills, one of the most isolated corners of Botswana.

Though it is possible to travel from the Aha Hills to Nokaneng via Gcangwa, the road is extremely sandy and should be considered as an alternative only after rain, when the surface is hard.

Backtrack to the Shakawe road and travel through Nokaneng to the turnoff to Tsodilo Hills, 10 km south of Sepupa. The road is very sandy and the 48-km journey can take up to three hours.

TSODILO HILLS

Rising unexpectedly above the sands of Ngamiland, the Tsodilo Hills are Botswana's best-known rock art site and national monument. They consist of four outcrops, referred to by the San as the Male, Female, Child and an unnamed hill. Depicted on rock walls and boulders are over 3 500 paintings of eland, rhino, giraffe, an elephant hunt, abstract patterns and, surprisingly, a fish. Five trails have been laid out on the Male and Female hills, where the largest concentration of paintings can be seen.

If they have time, Monument officers will accompany groups. Alternatively they can arrange San guides who know the location of the paintings, although they do not speak English.

You will find a number of basic campsites at the base of the hills, but these have no facilities. Water is obtainable from the Monument caretaker's office.

SHAKAWE

From Tsodilo Hills visitors have a choice of two routes to the Shakawe/Sehithwa road, both of which are extremely sandy. Situated alongside the Panhandle of the Okavango Delta, Shakawe is renowned for its excellent fishing – tiger fish, vundu and bream. It also offers fine birding, and notable species include the western banded snake eagle, the African skimmer (from July to December), Pel's fishing owl and coppertailed coucal. Large colonies of carmine bee-eaters nest in the river banks between August and November.

Several lodges in the area offer *mokoro*, boat and fishing trips. Drotsky's Cabins also cater for campers.

MAHANGO GAME PARK

The Mohembo border post between Botswana and Namibia is 16 km north of Shakawe. From here the road passes through the 24 462-ha Mahango Game Park, which is dissected by a proclaimed road from which two loops branch off. The riverside loop meanders alongside the Kavango River floodplains, where reedbuck and herds of red lechwe graze. The elusive sitatunga also occurs here, but uses the papyrus swamps as a hide-out and is rarely glimpsed. Mahango is home to a healthy elephant population and during the dry winter months they are often seen along the river, slaking their thirst.

The semi-circular route west of the main road leads through woodlands covering the dune landscape. Among the animals here are roan, sable, kudu, giraffe and Burchell's zebra.

With a bird list far in excess of 400 species, Mahango is one of the top birding spots in Southern Africa. Noteworthy species include the wattled crane, coppertailed coucal, greater swamp warbler, slaty egret and pinkthroated longclaw.

Except for two picnic sites situated along the riverside loop, the park (which is open only for day visitors) has no facilities. However, nearby Popa Falls Rest Camp is a convenient base from which to explore Mahango.

POPA FALLS

At Popa Falls, just north of Mahango, the Kavango River's journey to the Okavango Delta is blocked by a quartzite barrier that extends for about a kilometre across the river. Where the river breaches the reef, it splits up into a multitude of small islands and rushing channels to form a series of spectacular rapids.

Hidden amongst the lush riverine forest is the Popa Falls Rest Camp, with its rustic teak plank-and-thatch huts. Amenities include a field kitchen (the rest camp has no restaurant), a kiosk that stocks basic foodstuffs, and communal hot and cold water ablutions. Camping sites as well as facilities for day visitors are available beside the stream that runs through the rest camp.

CAPRIVI GAME PARK

Bounded in the west by the Kavango River and in the east by the Kwando River, the Caprivi Game Park is about 200 km long and 40 km wide. Plans are afoot to set aside core conservation areas along the two rivers, where the highest concentration of game tends to occur. The remainder of the park is very likely to be deproclaimed and managed as a multiple land use area.

Only the easternmost section of the game park alongside the Kwando River is currently open to the public. During the dry winter months, large numbers of game concentrate along the Kwando River, and it is not uncommon to see herds of elephant (several hundred strong) at Horseshoe Bend. Other species to be seen include buffalo, hippo, sable, kudu, eland, Burchell's zebra, impala, giraffe and tsessebe. Among the predators of the area are lion, leopard and wild dog.

The only available accommodation is a very basic campsite, which has no facilities, at Nambwa.

MUDUMU NATIONAL PARK

From Kongola Bridge at the Kwando River, the route continues on tar as far as the Sangwali turnoff; turn right here and continue for 31 km to Lizauli Traditional Village, where you can gain an insight into the culture of the region's people. Visitors are shown around the village and demonstrations are given of a ritual dance and also the use of traditional implements by a medicine man.

Mudumu's unfenced northern boundary is a little further. The 100 000-ha park is centred around a seasonal watercourse, the Mudumu Melapo, while the Kwando River, with its papyrus reedbeds, riverine forests and floodplains, forms the western boundary. The park is a sanctuary to three rare antelope species (sable, roan and oribi) and attracts over 400 elephants in the dry season. Burchell's zebra, impala, kudu, reedbuck, lion, leopard and wild dog also occur. The river, reedbeds and floodplains are home to hippo, crocodile, sitatunga and red lechwe.

The main attraction of the park is its incredible wealth of birds, and among the more than 400 species recorded to date are several with a limited distribution elsewhere in Southern Africa. Among the more notable species are the western banded snake eagle, African mourning dove, coppertailed coucal, Arnot's chat, yellowbilled and redbilled oxpeckers and coppery sunbird.

Facilities are limited to Lianshulu Lodge – a private lodge rated as one of the most outstanding accommodation establishments in Namibia – and the Nakatwa camping site. The area is best visited during the dry winter months as the tracks are generally impassable during summer.

From the southern boundary of Mudumu, continue for 21 km to the turnoff to Sangwali, a village with beautiful traditional buildings. You will reach the boundary of the Mamili National Park 13 km beyond the turnoff.

MAMILI NATIONAL PARK

This remote national park, cradled by the V-shaped arms of the Kwando and Linyanti rivers, is situated at the southernmost

Below: The Kwando/Linyanti River forms a natural boundary of the Mamili National Park, a seasonally inundated wetland.

point of the Caprivi Strip. During high floods, the river spills over the floodplains, inundating up to 80 per cent of the national park and leaving only the slightly higher forested areas of Nkasa and Lupala dry.

The 30 000-ha national park is home to one of the largest concentrations of buffalo in Namibia, while herds of elephant often congregate around Nkasa and Lupala during the dry winter months. Among the antelope you might see here are red lechwe, kudu, roan, reedbuck, impala and common duiker. Predators include lion, leopard and hyena.

The best time for game viewing is between late April and early August, while birding is especially rewarding in summer, when large numbers of migrant birds move into the area. (Bear in mind, however, that the roads are as a rule impassable during the rainy season.) Summer migrants include the squacco heron, yellowbilled kite, white and openbilled storks, greyhooded kingfisher, European, olive and carmine bee-eaters, and also the broadbilled roller.

From Mamili, continue to Katima Mulilo and the border post between Namibia and Botswana at Ngoma Bridge, northern access point to the Chobe National Park. The Victoria Falls (*see* page 111) are a mere 120 km away – a worthwhile detour.

CHOBE NATIONAL PARK

Covering over 1,1 million hectares, the Chobe National Park encompasses a variety of vegetation types, from mopane forest and brachystegia woodlands to floodplains. Equally diverse are its landscapes – these range from the panveld of the Nogatsaa

Below: In the last rays of the sun, the Okavango Delta glows in hues of red, orange and gold.

and Tchinga area to the riverine forests and marshes of the Linyanti and the fossil lake bed of the Mababe Depression.

With an estimated population of 35 000 elephants, Chobe is home to the largest concentration of this mammal in Africa. During the winter months herds of buffalo, numbering up to a thousand, congregate along the Chobe River. The riverine forest is home to the Chobe bushbuck, while the floodplains and adjacent grasslands support Africa's southernmost population of puku. Other species to be seen here include roan, sable, kudu, impala, waterbuck, reedbuck, giraffe and Burchell's zebra. The abundance of game attracts the full spectrum of large and small predators. Lion and hyena are especially plentiful in the Savuti area, which is famous for its annual zebra migration.

The park can be divided into four tourist areas, each with its own distinctive atmosphere and attractions. Serondela, in the north, is one of the most popular areas because of the great profusion of game that congregates along the Chobe River during the dry winter. Accommodation options range from a campsite at Serondela to two luxury lodges in the park, as well as a number of lodges in and around the town of Kasane.

In the west lies the Savuti area – a landscape of open grasslands, rocky outcrops, pans, the Savuti Channel with its distinctive dead trees, and the Savuti Marsh. The Channel has flowed sporadically during the past century, but has been dry since 1982, reducing the extensive marsh to a dust bowl. Savuti has a campsite and three lodges, the latter catering mainly for the more upmarket visitors.

Northwest of Savuti, the Linyanti River forms the boundary of the park for 7 km. Here riverine forests, reedbeds, marshes and floodplains merge to create a microcosm of the Okavango Delta. One of the least visited areas of the park, it attracts large herds of

covers 4 800 000 ha. A wildlife paradise, rivalled by few other game parks in Africa, the reserve can be divided into three areas: the permanently inundated delta, Chief's Island (both accessible by air) and the mainland areas of the Mopane Tongue and Mboma Island, the only areas accessible by vehicle.

Game abounds and includes hippo and crocodile in the rivers and red lechwe, tsessebe and waterbuck on the floodplains. Also to be seen here are elephant, buffalo, kudu, roan, sable, blue wildebeest, giraffe and Burchell's zebra. All the large predators, as well as a variety of smaller predators, are present.

Birdlife is prolific and the pans in the Xakanaxa area offer excellent opportunities for birding. Large colonies of herons, egrets, storks, ibises and cormorants breed at the Gcodikwe Heronry, accessible only by boat.

Popular areas in the reserve include the Khwai River with its spectacular floodplains, Dombo Hippo Pool, the Xakanaxa area, Dead Tree and Mboma islands, and Bodumatau.

Xakanaxa, Third Bridge, North Gate and South Gate all have camping sites. Five luxury lodges are situated within the reserve, with several more just outside Moremi's borders.

From Maqwee (South) Gate it is a 47-km drive on a very sandy track to Shorobe. The remaining 47 km back to Maun is tarred.

game during the dry winter months. Situated on the banks of the Linyanti River, the campsite is shaded by tall riverine forests.

The Nogatsaa/Tchinga area, about 60 km south of Serondela, is characterized by a wealth of pans set amongst mopane and broadleafed woodlands, grassland and bushwillow scrub. A great concentration of game converges around the pans during winter. Campsites are found at both Nogatsaa and Tchinga.

Proceed to Chobe's southern gate, Mababe, and continue for a further 50 km to reach North Gate in the Moremi Game Reserve.

MOREMI GAME RESERVE

Established in 1963 by the Batawana tribe, the Moremi Game Reserve was enlarged in the 1970s and again in 1991 and today

Top: *Namibia's perennial northern rivers, the Kavango and Kunene rivers, offer exciting opportunities for canoeing.*
Above: *The hauntingly beautiful cry of the African fish eagle is a familiar sound in the Okavango Delta.*
Right: *Leopard are often seen during the day in the mopane woodlands of the Moremi Game Reserve.*
Following pages: *The Moremi Game Reserve is home to large herds of buffalo which can most often be seen during the dry winter months.*

Zimbabwe and Western Zambia

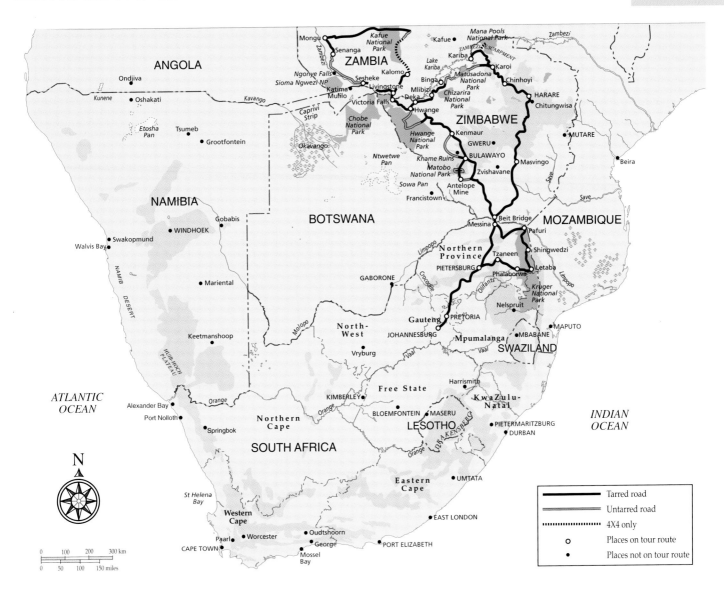

9

This tour combines some of Zimbabwe's archaeological, natural and man-made wonders with Zambia's remote Barotseland. It also takes in some of the great game parks of Zambia, Zimbabwe and South Africa, including the northern section of the Kruger, one of the least-visited areas of this renowned national park, before returning to Johannesburg – a trip of about six weeks.

Much of the 8 800-km tour can be completed in a sedan car, but the roads east of Chizarira National Park should ideally be negotiated in a four-wheel drive vehicle or a vehicle with high ground clearance. Although it is possible to travel on these roads in a sedan car during the dry season, it is inadvisable. Mana Pools National Park and a large part of the Kafue National Park are accessible only in a four-wheel drive vehicle.

Opposite: Buffalo grazing on Fothergill Island in Lake Kariba, just to the north of Matusadona National Park.

From Johannesburg, head to the north and travel towards Pietersburg, Louis Trichardt and Messina to reach the border post into Zimbabwe at Beit Bridge after 546 km. From here the road strikes northwest, passing West Nicholson (originally a mining centre) and Gwanda. Leaving the Great North Road north of Gwanda, the route swings west, continuing to Antelope Mine, and then north to Kezi and the Matobo National Park.

MATOBO NATIONAL PARK

This park covers 43 200 ha of hills and domes, weirdly shaped rock formations, valleys and woodlands. Focal point of the park is World's View, also known as Malindidzimu ('Place of Spirits'), with its sweeping vistas of the surrounding landscape. The stupendous view from here is matched by few others in Africa. Atop the massive granite dome is the grave of Cecil John Rhodes, who gave the country its pre-independence name.

Above: *Over countless aeons nature has sculpted the granite rocks of the Matobos into fascinating shapes.*

The overhangs and caves of the Matobos contain a wealth of well-preserved rock paintings. Among the best known caves are Nswatugi Cave with its polychrome giraffe, White Rhino Shelter, Gulubahwe Cave (featuring a 4,5-m-long snake) and Pomongwe Cave which has a site museum. These caves also used to be of spiritual significance to the Shona and Ndebele people.

The Matobos are renowned for their raptors, among them the world's largest concentration of the majestic black eagle. Other raptors recorded here include Wahlberg's, crowned and brown snake eagles, as well as sugar buzzard. The western section of the park has been set aside as a game sanctuary and among the many animals roaming the miombo woodlands are white rhino, giraffe, Burchell's zebra, kudu, sable, tsessebe, impala and klipspringer. The park also supports a large leopard population.

Accommodation ranges from luxury lodges and chalets to simple campsites at Maleme, Mtsheleli and Toghwana dams. In addition to game-viewing drives, visitors can go on guided walks or explore the area on horseback.

BULAWAYO

Situated about 32 km to the north of the Matobo National Park's northern boundary, Bulawayo, Zimbabwe's second largest city, is an important centre for the cattle ranching and mining industries. Laid out on the grid pattern of an imperial Roman settlement, it is characterized by several parks, and the streets are wide enough to allow a span of oxen to turn!

Be sure to visit the National Natural History Museum in Centenary Park. Among the exhibits are fascinating collections of minerals, the most comprehensive collection of birds in Africa, the largest collection of mammals in the southern hemisphere, as well as displays depicting the country's history.

Bulawayo has a variety of handicraft centres, among them the Mzilikazi Art and Craft Centre which is well known for its pottery, sculptures and basketry. Ndebele beadwork can be purchased at the Buhlaluse Project, while wall hangings are woven at Bulawayo Home Industries.

Also worth visiting is the Chipangali Wildlife Orphanage 24 km south of Bulawayo. Established to care for injured and orphaned animals, the orphanage is home to hundreds of mammals, birds and reptiles in need of care. Walkways through the orphanage afford close-up views of the animals.

The Khame Ruins, 22 km west of Bulawayo, are the most important ruins after Great Zimbabwe and a most interesting place to visit. The extensive city with its dry-packed stone walls was built between the 15th and 17th centuries, following the disintegration of Great Zimbabwe. Before setting off to explore the ruins, visit the site museum to gain an insight into the history of the place.

From Khame the route follows a main road to Tsholotsho and then continues along a minor road to Gwayi before heading for Kenmaur on the A8. Proceeding in a northwesterly direction, you will reach Halfway House and, 19 km beyond Gwayi River, the turnoff to the Hwange National Park.

HWANGE NATIONAL PARK

Hwange is the flagship of Zimbabwe's national parks and home to one of the largest concentrations of elephants in the world, estimated at as high as 30 000 animals. Covering 1,4 million ha, the park is a mosaic of grassy plains, mopane woodlands and pans supporting a wealth of game and prolific birdlife.

Hwange National Park is host to 107 mammal species, and among the 16 antelope species found here are kudu, eland, roan, sable, waterbuck and impala. Also present are large populations of buffalo, Burchell's zebra and giraffe. The abundance of prey attracts the full spectrum of predators, represented by no fewer than 25 species. Lion occur throughout the park, and they are especially common in the vicinity of Robins Camp. Other large predators include leopard, wild dog and spotted hyena. Game viewing is best from August to October, when the game tend to congregate around the waterholes and the grass cover is shorter than at the start of the dry season.

With a bird list of over 400 species, including several raptors, birding is most rewarding here. Species to keep an eye out for are the redwinged pratincole, Amot's chat and yellowbilled and redbilled oxpeckers. A variety of waders and water birds are attracted to the dams in the park.

Only the northern third of the park has been developed, the remainder being managed as a wilderness area, accessible only to tour operators. Accommodation in Main Camp (the park's administrative headquarters), Sinamatella and Robins camps ranges from lodges and cottages to chalets. Main Camp is the only rest camp that has a restaurant, and all three have campsites. The park also has four smaller camps.

A network of roads covering over 500 km links the numerous waterholes (some of which have viewing platforms), picnic sites and rest camps in the park.

From Main Camp, backtrack to the A8, from where it is an easy 195-km drive on tar to Victoria Falls.

VICTORIA FALLS

The awesome beauty of the Victoria Falls, also known as Mosi-oa-Tunya or 'The Smoke that Thunders', is matched by very few waterfalls in the world. Extending for about 1 700 m across the Zambezi River and 108 m at their highest point, the falls comprise the Devil's Cataract, Main Falls, Horseshoe Falls, Rainbow Falls, Armchair Falls and Eastern Cataract.

More than a dozen viewpoints on the edge of the gorge are linked by a walk through the Rain Forest. Starting at the statue of David Livingstone, the first white person known to have seen the falls, it winds through a lush forest of common red milkwood, African ebony ferns and orchids, ending at Danger Point which overlooks the Eastern Cataract.

For many visitors the ultimate reason for going to Victoria Falls is a white-water rafting trip down the Victoria Falls or Batoka gorges, or the 111-m-high bungi-jump (the highest commercial jump in the world) from Victoria Falls Bridge.

However, for the less adventurous, the area offers a host of other excursions, such as a visit to the Craft Village which depicts the culture and lifestyle of various ethnic groups, or a scenic drive through the 56 400-ha Zambezi National Park. Another very popular attraction in the area is the Zambezi Nature Sanctuary which incorporates a crocodile ranch.

For a bird's-eye view of the Victoria Falls, consider the 'Flight of Angels', a flight by aircraft or helicopter over the falls. Sunrise and sunset champagne cruises, as well as trips on the Upper Zambezi in river boats, inflatables, canoes and kayaks, are some of the other exciting activities offered.

Not to be missed is the Makishi dancing – visitors should enquire about venues at the tourist information office in Victoria Falls town. Various dances are performed by dancers in colourful costumes and masks, while the Makishi dancers keep the audience spellbound with their stilt walking. Alternatively, you can patronize the Explorers' Pub to listen to the stories of anguish of those who braved the white-water rapids of the Zambezi.

Accommodation at and near Victoria Falls ranges from luxury lodges and the lovely colonial-style Victoria Falls Hotel to the rustic cottages in the Zambezi National Park and campsites packed with overlanders in the town's rest camp.

From the town of Victoria Falls, take the arched Victoria Falls Bridge across the Zambezi River into Zambia. Constructed in 1905, the bridge spans the river for 198 m, offering breathtaking views of the falls and the gorge.

MOSI-OA-TUNYA NATIONAL PARK

Situated on the northern bank of the Zambezi River, the Mosi-Oa-Tunya National Park affords awe-inspiring views of the Victoria Falls, believed by many visitors to be even better than those on the Zimbabwean side.

A visit to the Victoria Falls Field Museum provides a most informative insight into how the falls were formed. Other things to see and do include a drive through the park, a cruise or canoe safari above the falls, and white-water rafting. Alternatively, consider the less nerve-racking 'Float of Angels' – a boat trip to the Boiling Pot – or a microlight flight over the falls.

Take a look at the Mukuni Craft Centre – the handicrafts are not only cheaper, but of a better quality than those on the Zimbabwean side. Nearby is the Maramba Cultural Village where the culture of the local people is portrayed.

From Mosi-Oa-Tunya, the route continues to Livingstone, where you can go to the museum and take a look at its excellent portrayal of the origins of the Bantu-speaking people. Also on display here is a collection of notes, letters and other items that belonged to David Livingstone.

Below: *Nyamandhlovu Pan is among the most popular game-viewing areas in Hwange National Park.*
Bottom: *Ivory Lodge is one of the many luxury lodges in the vicinity of Hwange National Park.*

Accommodation is available at several hotels and lodges in the area, the best known being the exclusive Tongabezi Lodge, approximately 17 km upstream of the falls.

From Livingstone, head in a northeasterly direction along the tarred T1 to Kalomo where a signpost indicates the turnoff to the Kafue National Park. The sandy access road and those in the southern section of the park, require a four-wheel drive vehicle and are negotiable during the dry season only. You will reach the southernmost entrance, Dumdumwenze Gate, approximately 75 km beyond Kalomo.

KAFUE NATIONAL PARK

Covering 2 240 000 ha, Zambia's largest and oldest conservation area is a patchwork of miombo and mopane woodlands and grassy plains. From Dumdumwenze Gate the track winds north through mopane woodland and then crosses the expansive grasslands of the Nanzhila Plains, renowned for their variety of antelope. Species to be seen here include Lichtenstein's hartebeest, sable, roan, eland and the elusive oribi. Also roaming the plains are impala, Burchell's zebra, blue wildebeest and a variety of predators, among them lion and cheetah.

You will reach the National Parks and Wildlife Service headquarters at Ngoma about 100 km after entering the park. To the north of Ngoma lies the Itezhi-Tezhi Dam, a 37 000-ha expanse of water on Kafue's eastern boundary. The dam offers excellent angling, birding and game viewing. Accommodation is available at three camps in the vicinity of the dam and also at the game management area adjoining the park.

Since no connecting road exists between the southern and northern sections of Kafue, you will have to take the route from Musungwa to Lukomeshi Post and then travel along the Mongu road to the Kafue River Bridge where you re-enter the park.

The northern section of the park is characterized by miombo woodlands and the vast Busanga Plains in the far north. Covering 75 000 ha, the plains are the habitat of the Defassa waterbuck (a subspecies that lacks the distinctive white ring on the rump), red lechwe and puku, while sitatunga inhabit the marshes. The waterways of the Kafue River are host to large numbers of hippo and crocodile. Also to be seen in this section of the park are elephant, buffalo, Burchell's zebra and the full spectrum of predators, including wild dog.

Several private camps and lodges are situated in the northern section of Kafue, but visitors should bear in mind that a four-wheel drive vehicle is necessary for most areas of the park. Also remember that much of the park is completely inaccessible between November and May, during and after the rainy season.

MONGU

From Kafue's western gate, Tatayoyo, the road leads to Kaoma and then through Barotseland, home to the Lozi people. You will reach Mongu, capital of Zambia's Western Province, 265 km beyond Kafue. Worth visiting is the museum at the Lozi king's dry-season capital, Lealui, a few kilometres northwest of Mongu.

Each year, as the level of the Zambezi River rises, the king moves in his royal canoe to the wet-season capital, Limulunga, with his followers trailing in their own canoes.

The route now continues south across the wide Zambezi floodplains to Senanga, where the tar road ends. Heading further southeast, you cross the Zambezi River by means of a ferry at Sitoti and then reach the village of Sioma. Should you plan on visiting the Sioma Ngwezi National Park, you would be well advised to obtain a guide or directions from the National Parks and Wildlife Service office in the village.

NGONYE FALLS

At Sioma the course of the Zambezi River is obstructed by a basalt dyke and the water leaps over it in a series of six 20-m-high horseshoe-shaped cascades strung across the width of the river. Despite the height of the falls, it is an impressive sight to see the immense volume of water pouring over the dyke. Ngonye Falls are best viewed by continuing to a turnoff about 2 km beyond Sioma, taking a dugout canoe to the eastern bank, and making your way upstream again. You can gain a different perspective of the falls by taking a boat excursion from Maziba Bay Lodge, a few kilometres downstream of the falls. The lodge overlooks a white beach and has luxury tented accommodation. A campsite offers alternative accommodation.

SIOMA NGWEZI NATIONAL PARK

Continuing further southeast, you reach the turnoff to the Sioma Ngwezi National Park a few kilometres beyond the falls. This park is Africa at its wildest and only bush-wise travellers should consider a trip here. The park has no facilities, and under no circumstances should you venture off the existing tracks.

This 500 000-ha national park is a mosaic of acacia and terminalia woodlands, teak forests, grasslands and pans. Owing to its proximity to Angola, poaching has been a problem, but with some patience you might chance upon elephant, tsessebe, sable, roan, giraffe and perhaps even a lion.

From the park, head towards Kalabolelwa and the Wenela border post, where you cross into Namibia near Katima Mulilo. From here the route continues to the Ngoma border post where you enter Botswana and can visit the Chobe National Park (see page 102). Proceed to the Kazungula border post, crossing into Zimbabwe and returning to the Victoria Falls.

From Victoria Falls, backtrack to the turnoff to the Tiger Mile Resort (formerly known as Deka Drum), a few kilometres before you reach the town of Hwange. The resort is situated about 47 km further along a narrow tar road.

DEKA, MLIBIZI AND BINGA

Tiger Mile, a popular angling resort, is situated at the southwestern end of Lake Kariba where the Deka River joins the Devil's Gorge. It has a fine reputation for tigerfish, barbel, bream and a variety of other angling species. Visitors can stay in rustic log cabins or at campsites. The resort also has a swimming pool.

The route to Mlibizi heads eastwards along a secondary road and then rejoins the tar road. Here it strikes in a northeasterly direction before swinging to the northwest. Mlibizi lies at the eastern edge of the Devil's Gorge, where the Zambezi River flows into Lake Kariba. It is the western terminus of the ferry service to Kariba, a 22-hour journey. Although angling is Mlibizi's main attraction, the area also offers excellent opportunities for birding, especially waterbirds. It is served by two hotels.

The next stop is the fishing resort of Binga, the second largest town of southern Kariba. The town was originally built as an administrative centre for the more than 100 000 Tonga people who were resettled in the area when the Kariba Dam started filling up in the early 1960s. Accommodation is available for tourists at the Binga Rest Camp, Kulizwe Lodge or Chilila self-catering cottages.

From Binga, backtrack to Manjolo and then follow the secondary road towards Siabuwa, keeping an eye out for the turnoff to the Chizarira National Park. The road to the park ascends very steeply up the escarpment and, although the park is accessible by sedan car, a four-wheel drive vehicle is essential during the rainy season, from November to March.

CHIZARIRA NATIONAL PARK

The attraction of this park, one of the most remote and least known in Zimbabwe, lies in its remarkable landscape. Situated atop the Zambezi Valley Escarpment, which forms its northern boundary for 30 km, the park's rugged scenery is characterized by deep gorges, well-wooded valleys and mixed acacia veld. From the escarpment it is an almost sheer drop of about 600 m to the Zambezi Valley far below.

Owing to the broken country and the dense vegetation, the most rewarding way to experience the panoramic grandeur and the wildlife of Chizarira National Park is by undertaking a four-day guided hiking trail conducted by Wilderness Safaris. Game species to be found here include elephant, lion, leopard, cheetah, buffalo and a variety of antelope, among them eland, sable, roan, tsessebe and impala. Of interest to birders is the taita falcon, a rare resident of Southern Africa.

Visitors to the park have a choice of rustic bush camps (with basic facilities) that must be booked *en bloc.* Alternatively, you can stay in the exclusive Chizarira Lodge just outside the park. Perched on the very edge of the escarpment, it has outstanding views over the park and the Zambezi Valley.

Beyond Chizarira the condition of the road deteriorates badly, making a four-wheel drive vehicle essential. Winding through Batonkaland, the road crosses the Luizilukulu, Sengwa and Ume rivers and passes rural settlements sporting huts built on stilts. This building style was originally used to avoid the floods of the Zambezi when the Batonka still lived in the area that is now inundated by Kariba. About 45 km beyond Siabuwa you will reach the turnoff to the Matusadona National Park. The road winding down the escarpment is negotiable only by four-wheel drive vehicles, and great caution should be exercised.

Above: *The gravel road traversing the Zambezi Valley Escarpment winds through wild and breathtaking scenery.*

MATUSADONA NATIONAL PARK

Situated on the shores of Lake Kariba, Matusadona is a scenic combination of secluded bays, inlets and grassy plains. The park is bordered in the west by the Ume River, and the spectacular Sanyati Gorge forms the eastern boundary. The northern third of the 1,5-million-ha park comprises the floor of the Zambezi Valley, while the remainder is characterized by the step escarpment and plateau. One of the highlights of a visit to Matusadona is the dramatic sight of the sunset over the lake.

The park is home to an abundance of animals, among them elephant, black rhino, buffalo, eland, sable and roan. Waterbuck graze on the floodplains, but the grassy plains are more likely to attract Burchell's zebra. Hippos are abundant in the lake, which also supports a large crocodile population.

Because of the ruggedness of the terrain, the park's road system is not extensive and the best way to see the game is to arrange a guided game-viewing walk. Another exciting option is a boat cruise along the shoreline, especially during the dry season (April to October) when the animals congregate along the water's edge. Not to be missed is a cruise up Sanyati Gorge with its sheer cliffs.

As elsewhere along the southern shores of Lake Kariba, tiger fishing is popular here. Sanyati Camp in the west of the park has three secluded camps exclusively for groups, as well as campsites at Tashinga, Sanyati West, Changacharire, Kanjedza and Jenje (the latter two without facilities). A number of luxury safari camps grace the shores of Matusadona, the best known being Fothergill Island Safari Lodge and Matusadona Water Lodge.

From the park, backtrack to the Karoi road. After crossing the Sanyati River the road ascends steadily to Karoi, from where it is an easy drive on tar to the town of Kariba.

Above: *Perched on a clifftop west of Matusadona National Park, the luxury Bumi Hills Hotel affords an expansive view over Lake Kariba.*

KARIBA

Also regarded as the 'Riviera of Zimbabwe', Lake Kariba offers a variety of attractions and activities. The duration of your stay here will ultimately be dictated by your interests, budget and the time on hand.

Situated on the northern shores of the 500 000-ha Lake Kariba, the resort town of Kariba boasts five marinas, and the activities available here are centred around watersports such as waterskiing, yachting and fishing. The dam is also an angler's paradise and many are lured here by the possibility of catching the ferocious tiger fish. Cruising is another popular activity – on board luxury cruisers for the well-heeled, while houseboats provide a less expensive alternative.

A great way of exploring the lake is to join a canoe trip along the inlets and bays of the lake shore. These trips afford excellent opportunities for bird watching and viewing game at close range. Canoe safaris are also conducted below the dam wall.

More sedentary activities at Kariba include a sunset cruise on the lake and a visit to the viewsite overlooking the 128-m-high dam wall. When full, the lake extends 282 km westwards and has a maximum width of 42 km. Also not to be missed is a visit to the church of St Barbara, built as a monument to Italian workers who died during the construction of the dam. Other attractions include the Crocodile Ranch and the Batonka Craft Village, where craftspeople can be seen at work.

From Kariba the road continues to Makuti and then winds down the escarpment to Marongora. Further along it crosses the Rukomechi River and after approximately 24 km you will reach Nyamepi Camp at Mana Pools.

MANA POOLS NATIONAL PARK

This 231 300-ha park fronts the Zambezi River and extends about 30 km southwards. It is named after four pools in an old course of the Zambezi River, the largest of which – Long Pool – is about 4 km long and 50 m wide. The park is ranked as one of the most outstanding game sanctuaries in Africa and during the dry winter it has the highest concentration of game in the entire continent. One of the main drawcards is the large herds of elephant, but also to be seen are herds of buffalo numbering over 500 animals, as well as eland, kudu, waterbuck, nyala, impala, Burchell's zebra, hippo and crocodile. Many predators are present too, including lion, leopard, wild dog and spotted hyena.

The road network is restricted to the Zambezi Valley, and visitors may walk in the park, but do so at their own risk. In recent years a number of visitors have been injured or killed in the park by wild animals, and extreme caution should be exercised when walking through the bush without a guide. Another way of enjoying the spectacular scenery and wildlife of the area is to join a canoe safari, ending at Mana Pools.

Facilities are limited to basic campsites along the Zambezi River and two private camps. Large areas of the national park are inaccessible during the rainy season, and the park is therefore closed between November and April. The numbers of visitors are strictly controlled, making it advisable to book well in advance.

HARARE

From Kariba it is an easy drive on tar to Zimbabwe's capital, Harare. The road initially winds through hilly terrain as it ascends the escarpment and then traverses the gently undulating plateau, passing through maize and tobacco farms.

At Chinhoyi it is worthwhile stopping at the Chinhoyi Caves at the foot of the Hunyani Hills. The passages and caverns of these limestone caves are dramatically lit with artificial light.

In Harare you can join up with Tour 10 which covers the Eastern Highlands and southeastern Zimbabwe (*see* page 121).

KRUGER NATIONAL PARK

From Harare, the road strikes south to Masvingo (*see* page 122) and then continues to the Beit Bridge border post with South Africa, a distance of about 580 km. The route then carries on to Messina and Tshipise, with its hot water mineral springs, and then heads east to Pafuri Gate, the northernmost entrance to the world-famous Kruger National Park. From here it is a further 70 km to the Punda Maria Rest Camp.

The Punda Maria/Pafuri area is a unique ecosystem in the park, but owing to its remoteness it is also one of the least visited areas. It is one of the few places in Southern Africa where tropical dry forest occurs – home to the rare suni. Several bird species reach the southern limit of their distribution here and Pafuri is a birder's paradise. Not to be missed while in the area is a visit to Thulamela, a citadel which was inhabited between the 15th and 17th centuries.

From Punda Maria continue southwards to Shingwedzi and Letaba rest camps. An interesting outing is to view the Goldfields Environmental Education Centre at Letaba, which houses the Elephant Hall where the tusks of six of the park's once famous Magnificent Seven can be seen. Various aspects of the elephant's life history are also displayed.

Because the Kruger covers nearly 2 000 000 ha, the duration of any visit here will depend on the amount of time and money available. From Letaba you can either continue further south or exit via Phalaborwa Gate. If you decide on the latter option, the Masorini Open-Air Museum is well worth a visit. This Late Iron Age site, which was inhabited until the 19th century, is sign-posted about 11 km before you reach Phalaborwa Gate.

From the iron-ore mining town of Phalaborwa the most direct route back to Johannesburg is via Tzaneen to Pietersburg on the N1. From here it is an easy 320 km on tar to Johannesburg.

Below: *Canoeing safaris are a popular activity on the Zambezi River at Mana Pools National Park.*

Left: *Bounded in the north by Lake Kariba, Matusadona National Park is home to large herds of buffalo.*
Above: *A highlight of the tribal dance performances at Victoria Falls is the masked Makishi dancers.*
Following pages: *The Victoria Falls are an awesome sight and one of the greatest natural wonders of the world.*

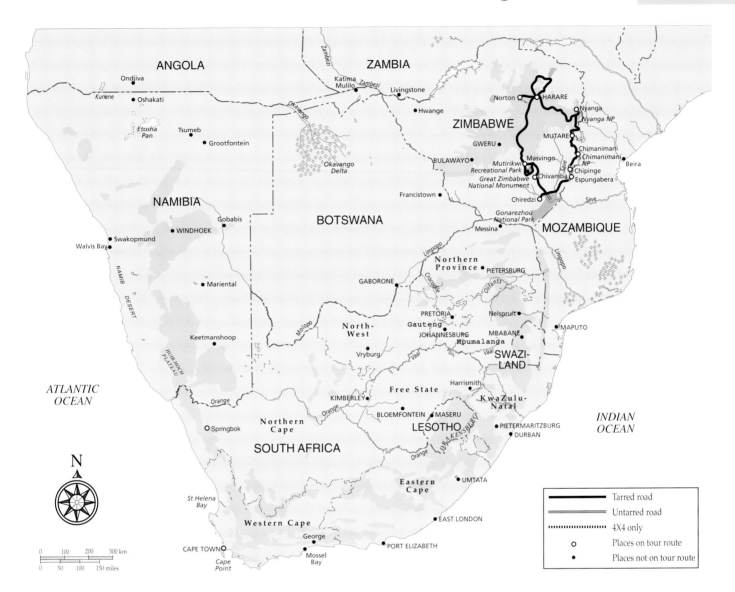

Starting in Harare, this tour combines the scenic and cultural attractions of Mashonaland with the wonderful wildlife of the Lowveld and the spectacular mountain scenery of the Eastern Highlands – a 300-km-long chain of mountains stretching all the way from the Chimanimani Mountains in the south to the Nyanga Mountains in the north.

Except for the section that goes through the Gonarezhou National Park, the entire trip can be done in a sedan car, although some of the gravel-surface back roads should be avoided by travellers in sedan cars during the rainy season, which is generally between November and March.

The length of the tour is approximately 2 000 km, and it will take about three weeks to complete.

Opposite: *The Chilojo Cliffs are a dominant feature of the Gonarezhou National Park in southeastern Zimbabwe.*

HARARE

Zimbabwe's capital, Harare, is characterized by its tree-lined avenues, modern skyscrapers and fine Victorian buildings. Before you set off to explore the city, call in at the tourist information bureau to find out more about its drawcards. Worth visiting are the Mbare Musika Market with its throngs of people, the National Botanical Gardens where most of the country's indigenous vegetation can be seen, and the National Gallery with its superb collection of Shona sculptures and other indigenous art. Another well-known city site is the Chapungu Sculpture Park, where more than 200 stone sculptures and a reconstructed Shona village can be viewed. Traditional dancing performances are held at the village on weekends.

Attractions in the area surrounding Harare include the fascinating balancing rocks at Epsworth (about 12 km south of Harare), the Domboshwa rock paintings and Lake Chivero

Top: *Great Zimbabwe is the most significant archaeological site south of the Sahara.*
Above: *Vervet monkeys become a dangerous nuisance when fed by visitors. They can inflict painful bites.*

Recreational Park (about 40 km southwest of Harare). The dam is popular with watersport enthusiasts, and the game park on its southern banks hosts white rhino, giraffe, sable, tsessebe, impala and Burchell's zebra. En route to the dam you might wish to visit the snake park and the Larvon Bird Gardens.

A rewarding day trip, the Harare/Shamva Loop Road meanders through scenic countryside, maize fields and citrus orchards to Mermaid's Pool and Ewanrigg Botanical Gardens. Covering some 285 ha, the park has an outstanding collection of cycads, aloes, succulents and cacti. A visit is especially satisfying in June or July when the orange and red flowers create a blaze of colour.

From Harare, the route strikes southwards to Chivhu and then continues to reach Masvingo, where the first permanent white settlement was established in Zimbabwe in 1890. Situated on a plateau of the middleveld, Masvingo is an important commercial and tourism centre. The turnoff to Great Zimbabwe is 5 km south of Masvingo on the Beit Bridge road. From here it is another 21 km on tar to the famous site.

GREAT ZIMBABWE

The historical and cultural significance of Great Zimbabwe is reflected in the country's name, flag and the national emblem which depicts the famous Zimbabwe birds. Great Zimbabwe (the name means 'Houses of Stone') is a national monument as well as a World Heritage Site. Covering an area of over 700 ha, the site is the largest of about 150 stone settlements in Zimbabwe and the most significant ruins in sub-Saharan Africa. The stone-walled city was built between the 13th and 14th centuries and became the royal city-state of the Shona-speaking Karanga Dynasty until its decline at the end of the 15th century.

Travellers should set aside at least four hours for a visit and, before setting off, look around the site museum to gain an insight into this ancient citadel. Among the items on display are the well-known Zimbabwe soapstone birds, numerous artefacts and an explanation of the different stonework techniques used in the construction of Great Zimbabwe.

The focal point of the site is the Great Enclosure, with its massive wall incorporating intricate geometric patterns, a narrow passage and a conical tower. Built without mortar, the wall has an average height of 7,3 m, a width of 5,5 m at the base and between 1,3 m and 3,6 m at the top.

In a nearby valley lies another complex, the Valley Enclosure, which consists of several structures. Overlooking the Great Enclosure is the Hill Complex – the oldest structures of Great Zimbabwe and the former court of the ancient royalty. The easiest way up to the Hill Complex is along the Ancient Ascent.

Facilities at Great Zimbabwe include a curio shop, a campsite with ablutions and a hotel.

From here the route continues along the Mutirikwi Circular Drive to the southern shores of Mutirikwi Recreational Park.

MUTIRIKWI RECREATIONAL PARK.

The 9 000-ha Lake Mutirikwi forms the focal point of this charming park which lies amidst splendid mountain scenery. It is a popular resort for yachting, boating, water-skiing, board-sailing and angling. A narrow strip of land along the southern shores forms part of the park, and visitors can stay here in thatched stone lodges, chalets or campsites. The park also has a restaurant, shop and swimming pool.

From Sikato Bay on the southern shore of the lake, the route leads past the 60-m-high dam wall, built in 1961 to provide water for the citrus and sugar estates of the Lowveld. It then continues along the Murray MacDougall Scenic Drive and through the picturesque Glenlivet Hills to the A9.

The game park, which is situated on the northern shores of the lake, can be accessed by travelling towards Masvingo for about 17 km, where the turnoff is signposted. The 4 800-ha game park is criss-crossed by a network of roads and among the animals which can be seen during a game-viewing drive are giraffe, Burchell's zebra, kudu, impala, eland, blue wildebeest and sable; hippo and crocodile inhabit the lake itself. Alternatively, the park can be explored on horseback.

From Lake Mutirikwi, follow the Birchenough Bridge road as far as the turnoff to Zaka, then take the road to Zaka. A short way beyond this settlement the road passes the ruins of a satellite structure of Great Zimbabwe and about 25 km further, near Chivamba, you will pass Runyani, another ruin site.

From Chivamba take the secondary road that gives access to the Manjirenji Recreational Park centred on McDougall Lake. The dam, in the course of the Chiredzi River, was built to irrigate 8 000 ha of farmland.

As you continue further to the southeast, the road passes into Zimbabwe's southern Lowveld, a cattle ranching and irrigation farming region. At the village of Chiredzi, the centre of the Lowveld's sugar cane farms, supplies and fuel can be replenished before you go on to Gonarezhou National Park.

The park is reached by taking a turnoff to the south at Nandi, east of Chiredzi. The route then continues along a gravel road to the park headquarters.

GONAREZHOU NATIONAL PARK

Bordering on Mozambique, Gonarezhou National Park covers 500 000 ha of mopani tree savanna, acacia woodlands, baobabs, pans and riverine forest. The Chipinda Pools region in the

northern section of the park is dominated by the dramatic red and white Chilojo Cliffs, which form a magnificent backdrop to the Runde River for about 32 km.

The name, Gonarezhou, means 'Refuge of the Elephant' and in the early 1990s the national park was home to about 8 500 elephants. Other species to be seen here include giraffe, buffalo, Burchell's zebra, Lichtenstein's hartebeest, roan, sable, nyala, waterbuck, suni and impala.

A long, devastating drought, which was broken early in 1993, resulted in the large-scale death of elephant and other animals from starvation. Over 380 elephants and 3 500 impala had to be culled, while large numbers of elephant calves and rare species of game were translocated. Artificial feeding programmes were also initiated. Although animal numbers are slowly recovering, it will still take some time before the park regains it former glory as a wildlife haven.

Some of the highlights of a visit to Gonarezhou include the striking Chilojo Cliffs, the Chivivira Falls, the imposing riverine

Below: *Gonarezhou National Park is a sanctuary to elephant and a variety of other game species.*
Bottom: *Visitors to Gonarezhou National Park can camp or stay in rustic thatched chalets.*

forest along the banks of the Runde River, and the Tamboharta and Machiniwa pans near the confluence of the Runde and Save rivers. These attractions, combined with the excellent birding, make a visit to the park a worthwhile experience. Among the 400 bird species you are likely to see here are the bat hawk, peregrine falcon, crested guineafowl, Pel's fishing owl, Böhm's spinetail and Narina trogon.

Accommodation in the northern section of the park is limited to campsites with ablutions. These campsites can be found at the main camp, Chipinda Pools, and at several other spots. Visitors, however, have to be self-sufficient in respect of all their needs, as no other amenities exist here.

Below: A large variety of indigenous and exotic plants is cultivated in the Bvumba Botanical Gardens.
Bottom: The fertile Honde Valley, south of the Nyanga National Park, is an important tea-producing area.

No direct road link exists between the Chipinda section of the park and Mabalauta, headquarters of the southern section. In the rainy season (November to March) the roads become inaccessible and the park is open only between May and October.

From Gonarezhou the route strikes north to Chisumbanje, running parallel to the Save River, and then turns off the A10 to the Gungunyana Forest, near Mount Selinda. Covering 940 ha, this impressive montane forest is the largest true rain forest in Zimbabwe. Among its attractions is the Big Tree, an enormous red mahogany tree with a height of 66 m and a circumference of over 15 m. Continue through Chipinge to the highland village of Chimanimani, gateway to the national park of that name.

CHIMANIMANI NATIONAL PARK

Most of the Chimanimani Mountains are conserved by this 17 100-ha park at the southern end of Zimbabwe's Eastern Highlands. The massif consists of three north/south ranges and the highest point, Kweza, rises to an altitude of 2 468 m. The mountains are characterized by dramatic scenery, deep gorges, sparkling streams and waterfalls, and are regarded as one of Southern Africa's most outstanding backpacking areas.

The park is accessible only on foot and from the park's base camp, Mutekeswane, it is a three- to four-hour walk along the ancient trade route between the interior and the Mozambican coast to the mountain hut on the plateau.

The Bundi River, high up on the plateau, has been stocked with trout and is popular with anglers. With some 300 bird species recorded to date, birding is rewarding and includes Gurney's sugarbird. Among the attractions in the north of the park are Tessa's Pool in the Zunguni River and the Bridal Veil Falls with its lace curtain cascading down the cliffs.

From the village of Chimanimani, the scenic route to Cashel is highly recommended. The route meanders through splendid mountain terrain and beautiful msasa *(Brachystegia)* woodlands to the fertile Tandai Valley, with its lovely waterfalls, before reaching the village of Cashel. The route continues westwards to Wengezi Junction and from there heads north along the A9 to Mutare and the Bvumba Botanical Gardens. Shortly before reaching the gardens, the road passes through the Bunga Forest Botanical Reserve – a tract of beautiful evergreen forest which can be explored along pathways.

BVUMBA BOTANICAL GARDENS

These splendid botanical gardens are centred around a series of streams and ponds on the summit of Bvumba Mountains, the Mountain of Mist. Pathways meander through the 32-ha landscaped garden with its lily ponds, well-kept lawns, streams and profusion of indigenous and exotic plants, but an area of 10 ha has been left in its natural state. From the gardens, visitors can enjoy expansive views over Mozambique to the east.

The Bvumba area is renowned for its rich diversity of butterflies and moths and the indigenous forests of the area also offer interesting possibilities for birders. Noteworthy species to

look out for include the Livingstone's lourie, Narina trogon, silverycheeked hornbill, Swynnerton's robin, Chirinda apalis and brier warbler. In order to absorb the magnificent scenery of the area, take a trip along the Burma Valley Drive, a 70-km circular route around Bvumba. Some of the amenities at the botanical gardens include campsites with ablutions, a tea-room, picnic sites and a swimming pool. More sophisticated accommodation is available at nearby establishments.

From Mutare the road ascends Christmas Pass and after 8 km turns off to Penhalonga. Gold was discovered here more than a century ago and the remote town has retained its turn-of-the-century character. Of interest here is a memorial to three nurses who walked from Beira to care for the miners in 1891, and also a corrugated iron church. Beyond Penhalonga the road winds its way across hills and valleys, passing the turnoff to Lake Alexander and, after crossing the Odzi River, reaches the turnoff to the Honde Valley with its tea plantations. It then continues to Mutasa and Juliasdale before reaching the Nyanga National Park.

NYANGA NATIONAL PARK

This remarkable park at the northern end of Zimbabwe's Eastern Highlands covers about 47 000 ha of pine trees, montane forest, granite hills, grassland and fynbos. It is renowned especially for

Above: World's View in the Nyanga Mountains affords the visitor endless vistas to the south.

its crisp mountain air, splendid mountain scenery and numerous breathtaking waterfalls, among them the 243-m-high Pungwe Falls and the 762-m-high Mutarazi Falls.

Walking to Mount Inyangani, at 2 593 m the highest point in Zimbabwe, is a very popular activity – the walk takes about an hour and a half from the car park. The rewards are great, with panoramic views into Mozambique and the deeply carved Honde and Pungwe Valleys.

The many streams in the park have been stocked with trout, and between September and May many hopeful anglers are lured here. Notable among the more than 300 birds recorded in the area are Livingstone's lourie, mottled and scarce swifts, blue swallow, brier warbler and the redfaced crimsonwing.

The park's road network provides access to viewpoints overlooking the Pungwe and Mutarazi falls, many dams and stone ruins. Accommodation is available at several hotels and lodges in the vicinity, as well as campsites with ablutions.

From the Nyanga National Park, the route back to Harare (along the A14 to Rusape and then the A3 via Marondera) passes through a landscape of striking rock formations.

125

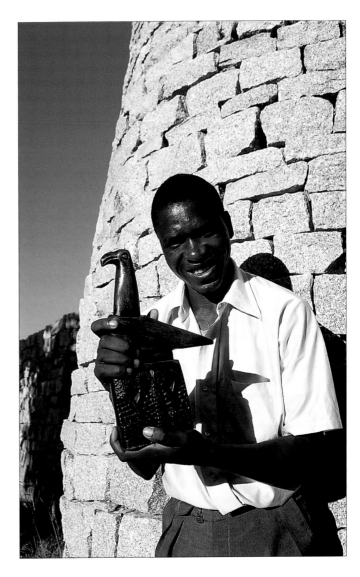

Left: *The Chimanimani National Park is criss-crossed by a network of footpaths for hikers to enjoy.*
Above: *Replicas of the famous Zimbabwe bird are sold at the Great Zimbabwe ruins.*
Following pages: *The Bridal Veil Falls cascade down the cliffs in the Eland Sanctuary of the Chimanimani National Park.*

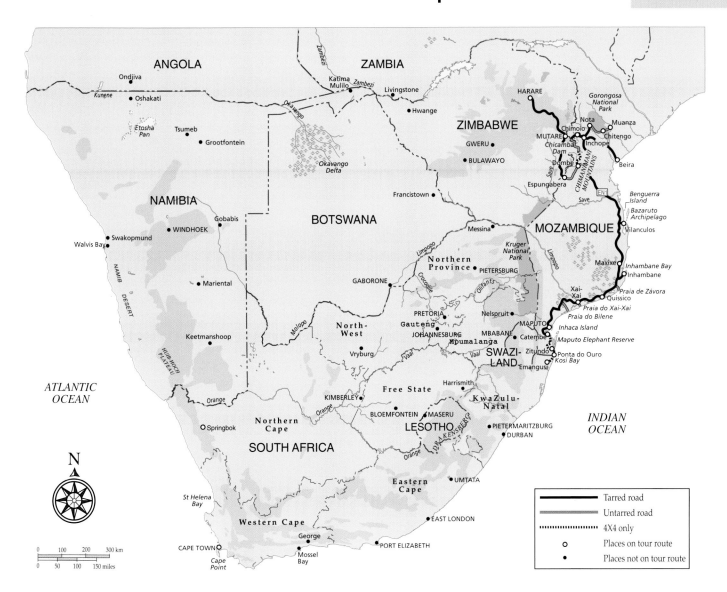

After many years of civil war, Mozambique is slowly rebuilding its economy and tourist infrastructure. This tour of central and southern Mozambique (starting from and returning to Harare in Zimbabwe) takes in some of the parks and reserves which are being rehabilitated and are open to day and overnight visitors.

While most of the route is on tar surface of varying conditions, several off-road sections are included. For this and safety reasons at least two four-wheel drive vehicles are advisable. Do not pick up hitch-hikers and beware of bogus roadblocks. The Mozambican landscape is littered with millions of mines and under no circumstances should you deviate from well-used tracks.

This tour is approximately 5 500 km long and it should take about six weeks to complete

Opposite: Local fishermen on a dhow off Benguerra Island, one of the islands of the Bazaruto Archipelago.

CHICAMBA DAM

From Harare, head for Mutare and then south on the A9 to Birchenough Bridge, Tanganda Junction (27 km south of Birchenough Bridge on the A16) and Mount Selinda, where you cross into Mozambique at Espungabera. The route passes some of the most dramatic scenery in Mozambique as it winds through the eastern foothills of the Chimanimani Mountains. Overlooking the Espungabera region is the 2 436-m-high Mount Binga, the highest point in Mozambique.

After about 105 km you reach the settlement of Dombe, where the road to Mavita deteriorates into a rough track. It is advisable to enquire about the condition of the track before setting off for Candeado and then north to Casa Msika Lodge on the western banks of the Chicamba Dam. Built in the course of the Revué River, the dam offers excellent opportunities for bream and bass angling, as well as birding. There is also a crocodile farm here.

131

GORONGOSA NATIONAL PARK

Covering about 5,3 million ha, Gorongosa is the best known of Mozambique's eight conservation areas – a mosaic of woodlands, termitaria islands of palms, winter thorn and fever trees and floodplain grasslands. Only three decades ago, the park was a sanctuary for 12 000 buffalo, 3 000 hippo and 2 000 elephant, as well as vast herds of antelope. However, do not expect to see large numbers of game – years of war and poaching have reduced the once-prolific game dramatically. Animals still occurring in small numbers include elephant, reedbuck, waterbuck, impala, red hartebeest, Burchell's zebra and several smaller mammals.

The park and surrounding areas offer excellent birding. After good rains Lake Urema and the floodplains attract a variety of waterfowl, pelicans, crowned crane, yellowbilled stork and flocks of redwinged pratincoles. Of special interest to birders is the greenheaded oriole, a species which can be seen only on the summit of Gorongosa Mountain to the north. The park was closed to tourists until 1996, when it was opened only to special interest ecotourists, such as birders. Camping is permitted in the renovated Chitengo Camp, while a campsite is being planned along the Púngoè River. An upmarket camp is envisaged at Bue Maria, further upstream along the Púngoè River.

From Chitengo, backtrack to Inchope and then continue to the settlement of Dondo. You will reach Beira 28 km further.

BEIRA

Also called the 'Heart of Mozambique', Beira is situated in the middle of Mozambique's 2 500-km-long coastline. It is a bustling commercial centre and much of the city's economic activity focuses on the harbour, the country's second largest port.

The city centre is characterized by late 19th-century and turn-of-the-century buildings. Among the noteworthy sites is Beira Cathedral, constructed with stones from the *Forteleza de Sofala*, the Portuguese fort built at Sofala in 1501. Other sites include the *Casa Portugal*, an excellent example of Beira's early colonial-style buildings, the Railway Station with its aerodynamic design, and the colourful *Mercado Central* (Central Market).

From Beira, follow the EN6 to Inchope and then head south on the EN1 to Save, a town on the Save River which marks the northern boundary of southern Mozambique. Continue across the Mozambique Plain to Vilankulo. Also known as Vilanculos, this coastal town 21 km off the EN1 is the springboard to the Bazaruto Archipelago. Transfers by skiboat can be arranged, or if you are not pressured for time you could consider a dhow trip.

BAZARUTO ARCHIPELAGO

Named after the largest of five islands off the coast of Inhassoro and Vilankulo, this archipelago is a tropical paradise of unspoilt beaches, coral reefs and the turquoise waters of the Mozambique Channel. The other islands in the archipelago, Benguerra (Ilha de Santo Antonio), Magaruque, Santa Carolina (formerly known as Paradise Island) and Bangue (the smallest island), as well as eight reefs, fall within the Bazaruto National Park.

Above: *Angling is one of the main attractions of Benguerra Island along the coast of Central Mozambique.*

Accommodation and amenities include six-bed chalets with *en suite* shower and toilet, a restaurant, bar and swimming pool.

From Casa Msika the route strikes north to the EN6 and then continues to Chimoio, capital of Manica Province. Located on the Beira Corridor, Chimoio is an important commercial centre and the country's fifth largest town.

The route now continues in an easterly direction on the Beira road for approximately 64 km to Inchope and then north for about 42 km to the turnoff leading to the Gorongosa National Park. Travelling along the road to Muanza, you will reach the park's entrance gate after about 11 km, and the park's head-quarters at Chitengo is some 17 km further.

The archipelago is rated as one of the top billfishing areas in the world, and game fish include the king mackerel, wahoo, giant kingfish and dorado. Saltwater fly-fishing is also becoming increasingly popular, but scuba diving and snorkelling are the two major drawcards of Bazaruto. Two Mile Reef, about 3 km off the gap between Bazaruto and Benguerra islands, is a favoured spot offering excellent snorkelling at low tide on the landward side of the reef and scuba diving on the seaward side. Scuba dives range from 12 m to 26 m, with each dive site presenting unique opportunities. Other exciting watersports include boardsailing, water-skiing and hobiecat sailing.

Bazaruto Archipelago also has much for naturalists to enjoy, and chief among its many wildlife attractions is the possibility of spotting a dugong or whale shark. Among the 180 bird species recorded to date are rarities such as the crab plover; other species include flamingoes, petrels, waders and osprey.

The freshwater pools on Bazaruto are home to crocodiles, while red duiker, bushbuck, samango monkey, red squirrels and bush-babies are among the 14 mammal species occurring on the island.

The islands of Bazaruto, Benguerra and Magaruque all have first-rate accommodation and services to ensure that your holiday will be an unforgettable one.

INHAMBANE

From Vilankulo, the route continues in a southerly direction along the EN1 to Inhambane, the capital of the province of that name. Situated on the landward side of a long sand spit, it is an attractive harbour town characterized by coconut palms, dhows and a distinctly Oriental atmosphere. Among the interesting city sights are the Cathedral of Our Lady of

Above: The hotel on Magaruque Island comprises double rooms and beach bungalows.

the Conception, built over two centuries ago, the former Palace of the Governor, and the *Grafica Sul do Save*, where old-fashioned printing presses are still used today.

A number of good scuba-diving and snorkelling spots are situated along the peninsula. Not to be missed is a trip by dhow across Inhambane Bay to the town of Maxixe.

XAI-XAI

En route to Xai-Xai along the EN1, you will pass the turnoff to Praia de Závora (the turnoff is not signposted), a marvellous angling and snorkelling spot. Accommodation is available in bungalows or houses, while camping is also permitted.

Beyond Inharrime the road crosses Lake Poelela and continues through Mozambique's 'Lake District' to Quissico, where the beach and lagoons can be accessed along an 11-km track. About 67 km further the road reaches the village of Chidenguele which is set amidst a string of lakes.

Xai-Xai, the capital of Gaza Province, lies on the banks of the Limpopo River. From here it is 10 km to Praia do Xai-Xai, a popular coastal resort and a mecca for ski-boat angling. The reefs have wonderful scuba diving and snorkelling opportunities at depths ranging from 2 m to 25 m. The beach and tidal pool at Wenela, 2 km south of the resort, offer safe swimming, but because of the dangerous currents you should not be tempted to swim in the tunnel which links the pool to the sea. A number of accommodation establishments in the area cater for visitors.

BILENE

From Xai-Xai, the route winds inland and at Macia the turnoff to Praia do Bilene, also known as San Martino, is signposted. This resort, reached after a further 33 km, lies alongside the 27-km-long Uembje Lagoon where it is quite safe to go for a swim. Accommodation ranges from lagoonside campsites to a hotel and self-catering cottages.

The route from Macia continues along the EN1 and you will reach Maputo after about 146 km.

MAPUTO

Mozambique's capital city, Maputo, consists of an assortment of dilapidated high-rise structures contrasting with beautiful Portuguese colonial buildings. Since the residential area forms part of the city centre, Maputo becomes even more lively after dark as people take to the streets, cafés and pubs.

Before setting off to explore the city, it would be useful to call in at the tourist information bureau. When moving around Maputo, avoid being conspicuously a tourist, as they are often the targets of pickpockets and thieves.

Among the city sites worth visiting is Independence Square, where the ornate *Cathedral de Senhora de Conceicão*, the neo-classical *Conselho Executivo* (City Hall) and also the Tunduru Botanical Gardens can be viewed. Adjacent to the botanical gardens is the *Casa do Ferro*, a prefabricated building designed by Gustav Eiffel who also designed the famous Eiffel Tower in Paris. A most enjoyable experience is a trip to the bustling central market at the *Mercado Municipal*. Be very cautious though – the dense crowds of people make this an ideal place for pickpockets to target unsuspecting tourists.

Below: The Maputo Elephant Reserve is a mosaic of forested dunes, grasslands and marshes.

Maputo has several museums; don't miss the Museum of the Revolution where the history of Frelimo's armed struggle against Portuguese rule is portrayed on four floors.

Accommodation in Maputo ranges from the graceful colonial-style Polana Hotel and the luxury Cardoso to more modest establishments, while hundreds of restaurants and snack bars are dotted around the city, among them Maritimo (excellent seafood), Pequim (meat and fish) and the Piri Piri (chicken and prawns). Also excellent for seafood is the Costa do Sol, at the end of the Marginal (Marine Drive).

INHACA ISLAND

Situated a mere 24 km off the coast of Maputo, Inhaca Island can be reached by air (a 15-minute flight), by speedboat (a 45-minute ride) or by taking the government ferry (a three- to four-hour trip). The main attraction of this island, with its pristine beaches and palm trees, is undoubtedly watersport. Snorkellers and scuba divers can explore the magnificent coral reefs and numerous wrecks, and other activities in and around the water include deep-sea angling, saltwater fly-fishing, paddle-skiing, water-skiing, windsurfing and pedal boating.

A tour of the Biology Museum with its fascinating collection of coral is worthwhile, as is an excursion to the lighthouse near the northern tip of the island. Arrangements can be made with the Inhaca Hotel for a boat trip to Portuguese Island, just north of Inhaca village, with its outstanding coral reefs. Alternatively, you can walk to the island at low tide.

Visitors can either stay at the Inhaca Hotel or camp on Inhaca or Portuguese Island. Not to be missed is a seafood meal at Lucas' Restaurant, a name which is synonymous with Inhaca, at the market in Inhaca village.

MAPUTO ELEPHANT RESERVE

By far the easiest way to get from Maputo to Ponta Malongane is to take the ferry to Catembe, which is situated on the southern shores of Maputo Bay. The ferry operates regularly and the trip takes approximately 15 minutes. Restaurante Diogo, near the ferry terminal in Catembe, is well known for its prawns and has become quite an institution.

From Catembe, the route passes through Bela Vista, crossing the Maputo River a short way before reaching Salamanga. At this point the road deteriorates into a sandy track, negotiable only in a four-wheel drive vehicle.

A few kilometres beyond Salamanga you will reach the turnoff to the headquarters of the Maputo Elephant Reserve. Here you can obtain directions to the southern entrance gate of the reserve from where you can proceed to Zitundo, a town overlooking Lake Satine ou Sotiba. The elephant reserve is currently open to day visitors only, and overnight camping is strictly prohibited.

Covering about 50 000 ha, the reserve comprises a patchwork of golden beaches, forested dunes, grassland floodplains, wood-lands, mangrove swamps and lakes. The land was originally set aside in 1932 as a sanctuary for the elephants that once occurred

here in large numbers. Because of the civil war in Mozambique their numbers decreased alarmingly, while the 65 white rhino relocated from the then Umfolozi Game Reserve in 1967 were totally destroyed. The Futi River, a fossil river, provides an ecological link between the reserve and the Tembe Elephant Park in northern KwaZulu-Natal and was used for centuries by the elephant to migrate into the Tembe area. The decrease in the number of elephants, however, prompted the Natal conservation authorities to fence off the northern boundary of the Tembe Elephant Reserve in 1989. An estimated 150 elephants inhabit the Maputo Elephant Reserve, while Tembe Elephant Park has a population of about a hundred.

Despite the large-scale poaching and a lack of management during the country's civil war, the Maputo Elephant Reserve was singled out as one of the world's 200 global diversity sites at the Earth Summit in Rio de Janeiro in 1992.

In late 1996 the Mozambican government approved a controversial tourism project proposed by an American company, Blanchard Mozambique Enterprises. In terms of this multimillion-rand project, BME will obtain a concession area of over 230 000 ha, which includes 400 ha on Inhaca Island and stretches southwards to the South African border. The development will include a marina, luxury housing, game lodges, floating casinos and a railway line.

As all beach driving in Mozambique is strictly forbidden, the route from Zitundo continues directly to Ponta do Ouro. At the crossroad turnoff to Ponta do Ouro, bear left and travel through thick sand for about 6 km to reach Ponta Malongane.

Above: *You can launch a diving boat at Ponta Malongane on Mozambique's southern coast to explore the offshore reefs.*

PONTA MALONGANE

Overlooking a sheltered beach, Ponta Malongane and nearby Ponta do Ouro have become increasingly popular in the last few years. The resort at Ponta Malongane nestles alongside coastal dune forest and offers exciting diving opportunities, ranging from shallow coral dives to 36-m dives. Well-known dive sites include Bass City, the Ridge and Pinnacles, famous for its sharks. Accommodation ranges from campsites (with electricity) to basic rondavels and fully-equipped chalets.

To travel from Ponta Malongane to Ponta do Ouro, follow the route that winds inland. You will reach the turnoff to Ponta do Ouro after about 8 km.

PONTA DO OURO

This delightful resort, situated close to the South African border, is sheltered by a protected bay flanked by high forested dunes. It offers safe swimming, rock and surf angling and excellent game-fishing. Another attraction is the superb scuba-diving at well-known reefs such as Checkers and Fingers. Accommodation ranges from cabanas at the Ponta do Ouro Motel to huts, luxury chalets and campsites.

At Ponta do Ouro this tour joins up with Tour 5 (*see page 69*) which ends in Johannesburg. From here the route continues for another 456 km to the Beit Bridge border post between South Africa and Zimbabwe and then to Harare, 570 km further.

Top: A clownfish, one of the many colourful tropical fish species that divers and snorkellers can see on the reefs along the southern coast of Mozambique.
Above: The easiest way to travel from Maputo to the popular diving spots further south is to take the Catembe ferry.
Right: Magaruque Island is characterized by extensive sandbanks and, together with Bazaruto and Benguerra islands, was once part of the Mozambican mainland.
Following pages: Grasslands, forested dunes, lakes and pristine beaches merge at Ponta Malongane along the coast of southern Mozambique.

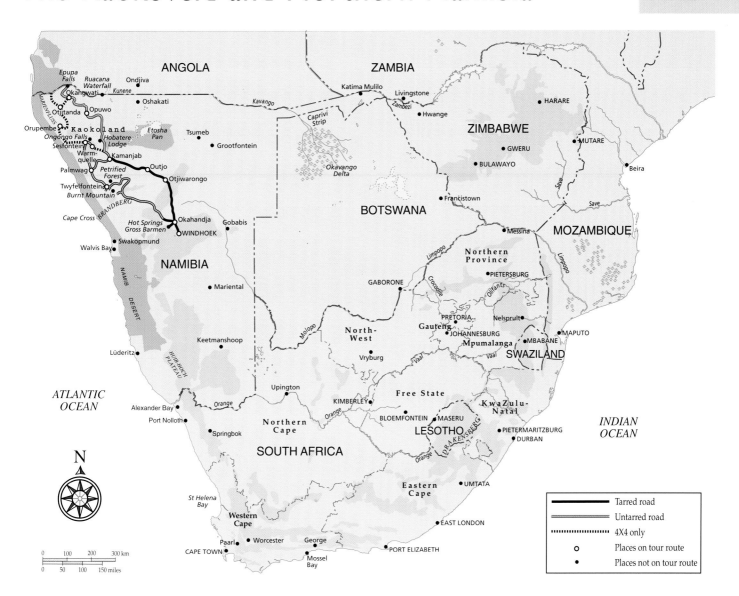

The Kaokoveld in northwestern Namibia is a wilderness of rock, plains and rugged mountains. Often called Southern Africa's last wilderness, it is a refuge to desert-dwelling elephants and black rhino. It is also home to the Himba people – Herero-speaking pastoralists who still pursue their traditional way of life. Though the Himba are friendly people, ignorance and disregard for their customs can result in misunderstanding and resentment. Always treat them with due respect, and obtain their permission and negotiate payment before taking their photographs.

In recent years the roads in the Kaokoveld have been improved considerably and it is now possible to travel all the way to Epupa in a sedan car. All roads except the C35/C41 and the D3700 from Opuwo to Epupa Falls are negotiable only with 4x4 vehicles.

Opposite: This informal campsite in the Kaokoveld is sheltered from the wind by a large sandstone outcrop.

Always stay on existing tracks and do not travel up or down river courses. The Kaokoveld is a sensitive area and tracks can remain visible for 80 years or more. Strictly no entry is allowed to the Skeleton Coast National Park other than through the official entrance gates. This 3 000-km tour takes two to three weeks.

KAMANJAB

Starting in Windhoek (*see* page 151), take the B1 north through Okahandja and Otjiwarongo to Outjo and then continue to the farming settlement of Kamanjab. About 5 km before reaching Kamanjab, an inconspicuous track turns off to Peet Albert Koppies, a hillock to the north of the road. From the parking area a path meanders among the rocky outcrops – the site of Namibia's second largest concentration of rock engravings. More than 1 000 engravings have been carved into the rocks, but they are not as finely executed as those at Twyfelfontein (*see* page 144).

Above: Himba girls wear plaits until adolescence and adorn themselves with a variety of body ornaments, including necklaces made from wire beads, copper bracelets and a conch which is passed on from mother to daughter.

HOBATERE

The route continues north from Kamanjab along the Ruacana road for 69 km to the turnoff to Hobatere Lodge, the lodge being about 15 km further. Covering 35 000 ha of woodlands and plains interspersed with granite outcrops, Hobatere is home to a vast array of birds and game. Animals include elephant, giraffe, Hartmann's mountain zebra, eland, gemsbok and springbok. Predators of the area are lion, leopard and cheetah.

Guided game-viewing drives are conducted in the mornings, as well as guided walks tailored to suit any particular group. After dinner, visitors can go on a night drive with a spotlight in search of nocturnal creatures. The lodge also arranges special day trips to the western reaches of the Etosha National Park, an area closed to the general public.

Guests at Hobatere are accommodated in thatched cottages with *en suite* facilities. The lodge has a thatched dining room and bar, as well as a swimming pool.

EPUPA FALLS

From Hobatere the road strikes north into Kaokoland and then heads west to Opuwo, the capital of the Kunene region. This is the last filling station, so before continuing ensure that fuel supplies are sufficient for the 800-km journey that lies ahead. Continuing through mopane veld, the road to the Himba settlements of Otjivize and Okangwati is usually in a fair to good condition, but you should nonetheless exercise caution at the causeways. A visit to the traditional Himba demonstration kraal, 12 km from Okangwati, provides a fascinating insight into the lifestyle, culture and customs of the Himba people.

Large numbers of Himba people have settled around Opuwo. Although there are semi-permanent settlements at Orupembe, Purros and elsewhere in Kaokoland, the Himba are pastoralists and they move about constantly with their herds in search of grazing. Their distinctive beehive-shaped huts are built from mopane saplings covered with a mixture of clay and cow dung. The Himba are striking in appearance and the men are often said to resemble the Maasai of East Africa. Himba women cover their bodies with butterfat mixed with powdered oxides and herbs, giving their skin a rich, gleaming ochre colour.

Proceed towards Omuhonga, from where the road continues through mopane woodlands, passing the occasional Himba kraal. Since the Himba are nomadic, their kraals often appear abandoned, but household articles should never be removed.

About 60 km beyond Omuhonga, the breathtaking Epupa Falls suddenly come into view. Here the Kunene River splits into a series of channels, separated by palm-clad islands. The main fall in the southernmost channel plunges 68 m into a narrow gorge and a series of waterfalls, cascades and cataracts can be seen across the width of the river. Adding to Epupa's magical scenery are huge baobab trees clinging tenaciously to the sides of the gorges. The beauty of Epupa is best appreciated by following a well-defined footpath along the slopes of the hill overlooking the gorge. Epupa has been identified as a possible site for Namibia's second hydro-electric plant, and in a few years' time this magnificent site might well be under water.

Along the river are campsites with braai facilities, cold showers and flush toilets. The two tented lodges in the area cater for guests on a full-board basis.

MARIENFLUSS

After backtracking to Okangwati, turn southwest, continuing past the Himba settlements of Etengwa, Okauwa, Otjitanda and Otjihende to Van Zyl's Pass. From the viewpoint (situated just north of the pass' summit) you can enjoy expansive panoramas onto the plains and the Marienfluss, a 50-km-long valley.

Little maintenance is carried out on the pass and after summer rains it is often difficult to negotiate. Due to the steep gradient, it is advisable to engage low range, allowing the engine to run against its own compression. The road twists vigorously as it wends its way down the pass, losing some 800 m in altitude.

The track now heads in a northwesterly direction to the Marienfluss, bounded in the west by the Hartmann Mountains. To the east the almost vertical cliffs of the towering Otjihipa Mountains rise 1 400 m above the valley floor.

During years of low rainfall the sandy plains are barren and stark, but after good rains they are covered in lush green grasslands that turn golden-yellow as the grass begins to wither. A conspicuous feature of the Marienfluss are the mysterious fairy circles – circular patches of earth devoid of vegetation. Their origin has yet to be explained. A community campsite is situated at Otjinhungwa, on the banks of the Kunene River. Crocodiles lurk in the water, making it particularly inadvisable to swim here, but you should exercise caution along the entire river.

PURROS

To reach Purros, backtrack for about 50 km and then head for the Rooidrom (Red Drum), continuing to the Himba settlement of Orupembe. From here the track traverses the gravel plains in a southwesterly direction, with the Etendeka Mountains – a table-top range consisting of horizontal layers of lava overlying layers of sandstone – prominent to the east. The track then swings towards the southeast to Purros.

Situated close to the Hoarusib River, Purros has a small community of Herero people and nomadic Himba pastoralists. Nearby, at the junction of the Hoarusib and Gomatum rivers, is Ngatutungwe Pamwe Campsite. Amenities at the campsite, run by the Purros community, include braai areas, firewood, showers and toilets. Make arrangements with the supervisor of the campsite to hire guides for an interpretative walk, focusing on plants used by the Himba and Herero people; you may also encounter the desert-dwelling elephants that frequent the area. Other game species to be seen include giraffe, gemsbok, kudu and ostrich.

Top: The landscape around Palmwag is dominated by flat-topped mountains and rock-strewn plains.
Above: The Epupa Falls on the Kunene River in northern Namibia are among the country's most spectacular attractions.

143

SESFONTEIN

Heading in a southeasterly direction, the route now traverses the spectacular Giribes Plains. These plains are especially beautiful after good summer rains, when herds of springbok and gemsbok are attracted to the rippling grasslands.

After crossing the plains, you will reach Sesfontein – a fertile oasis in the harsh Kaokoveld landscape. The green pastures and palm trees contrast sharply with their arid surroundings. Several springs surface here, providing an abundant supply of water for irrigation farming of wheat, lucern and tobacco.

The focal point of this settlement is the historic fort, built by the German army in 1905/6. The fort has been converted into a lodge, its rooms (complete with *en suite* facilities) arranged around a central courtyard. Amenities include a restaurant and bar (in the old officers' mess) and a swimming pool. Campsites are available, as is a filling station.

ONGONGO FALLS

From Sesfontein the route continues to Palmwag, reaching the settlement of Warmquelle after approximately 21 km. Keep an eye out for a rudimentary signboard indicating the turnoff to the Ongongo Falls as you enter the settlement. You will reach the falls about 6 km further.

Arriving at Ongongo after a few days of travelling through the Kaokoveld can only be described as sheer bliss. Lukewarm water cascades over a tufa waterfall into a crystal-clear pool, creating one of the most idyllic spots in Kaokoland. Ongongo has a community campsite with cold showers and toilets.

KHOWARIB SCHLUCHT

The turnoff to Khowarib Schlucht is signposted about 11 km beyond Warmquelle on the road to Palmwag. Perched on the high southern bank of the Hoanib River, the Khowarib community campsite offers accommodation in traditional Himba and Damara huts, and campsites are also available.

Heading east, the route follows the narrow gorge sculpted through the mountains by the Hoanib River for about 23 km. You will have to cross the river several times, and the soft, loose sand necessitates engaging a low gear.

Along the first 40-km stretch you will come across several patches of axle-deep silt which must be negotiated in four-wheel drive. The 'waves' formed before you by the talcum dust of these areas can engulf the vehicle completely. From the Kamdescha veterinary control point (63 km from the Khowarib campsite) it is another 20 km to the Kamanjab/Ruacana road.

PALMWAG

From Kamanjab, take the scenic road over the Grootberg to Palmwag. Most visitors are attracted to Palmwag in the hope of catching a glimpse of Damaraland's famed desert-dwelling elephant and black rhino. Situated on a tributary of the Uniab River, the lodge at Palmwag overlooks a spring where elephant frequently come to drink. Far more elusive are the black rhino, and chances of seeing them are best during the early mornings and late afternoons. Other species of game you might chance upon are giraffe, kudu, gemsbok, springbok and ostrich.

With landscapes ranging from expansive plains (dotted with clumps of euphorbia) and boulder-strewn slopes to the conical peaks and the flat-topped mountains of the Grootberg range, the scenery around Palmwag is dramatically beautiful. Well worth visiting is Van Zyl's Gat, a deep pool in the bed of the Uniab River, and the striking Auob Canyon. The entire area to the west of the Palmwag/Sesfontein road is a concession and a permit must be obtained at the lodge before entering the area.

Accommodation at the lodge consists of reed-and-thatch bungalows, and campsites are also available. Amenities include two swimming pools, a restaurant and a kiosk. Fuel is obtainable at a filling station at the veterinary control post.

TWYFELFONTEIN

The route from Palmwag follows the road towards Khorixas and then continues along a signposted road to Twyfelfontein. The Aba-Huab campsite, situated just a few kilometres from Twyfelfontein, is a convenient base for exploring the area. It has A-frame shelters, braai facilities and hot water ablutions.

With some 2 500 petroglyphs, Twyfelfontein has the largest concentration of rock engravings in Southern Africa. Among the more interesting engravings carved into the sandstone rocks are depictions of two large rhinos, an elephant and a lion with a paw print at the end of its L-shaped tail (*see* photograph on page 146). You will also see several engravings of antelope and animal spoor.

An unusual feature is the nearby Burnt Mountain – a flat-topped mountain that glows orange, red and brown in the early morning light. The Organ Pipes, a mass of angular dolerite columns, can be seen in a small gorge to the left of the road.

Below: Axle-deep silt enshrouds a four-wheel drive vehicle in a cloud of fine dust in the Khowarib Schlucht.

PETRIFIED FOREST

Instead of backtracking to the Khorixas/Torra Bay road, follow the district road to the farm at Blaaupoort and then head northeast to the C39 and the Petrified Forest. Covering an area of about 2,5 square kilometres, numerous petrified trees are scattered about a sandstone outcrop on the northern bank of the Aba-Huab River Valley. Research has shown that the trees did not grow here, but were washed downstream by floods. One particularly large tree has a partially-exposed trunk of 30 m with an estimated circumference of 6 m. Four species of trees belonging to the family of cone-bearing plants have been identified. Shaded picnic tables are provided at the entrance gate.

Tempting as it might be, do not remove even a small piece of the petrified wood – the site is a national monument and offenders will be prosecuted.

Khorixas Rest Camp is situated just before you enter the town of Khorixas, an important administrative centre for the area. The rest camp has bungalows and campsites, as well as a restaurant, lounge, bar, curio shop and swimming pool.

BRANDBERG

From Khorixas the route continues in a southerly direction to the Brandberg, renowned for its rock paintings. Best known among the more than 43 000 rock paintings on the mountain is the so-called White Lady frieze in the Tsisab Ravine, reached after a 60- to 90-minute walk from the parking area at the end of the district road. Contrary to popular opinion, the central figure is a male and does not depict a person of Egyptian, Cretan or

Above: The bizarre-looking Welwitschia mirabilis *is endemic to the Namib Desert in Namibia.*

Mediterranean origin. Many other rock painting sites are found in the immediate vicinity of the White Lady frieze.

These paintings form an important part of Namibia's heritage and should under no circumstances be touched or damaged. Also, do not spray water or any other liquid onto them.

Rising more than 2 000 m above the surrounding plains is the 2 579-m-high Königstein, the highest point in Namibia. Ascending Königstein is a very popular backpacking excursion, but, due to the demanding terrain and the lack of water, this should not be attempted unless you are accompanied by someone familiar with the area.

GROSS BARMEN

The return route to Windhoek goes through Uis (where tin was once mined) to Omaruru and then on to Wilhelmstal, where you reach the Swakopmund/Okahandja main road, the B2. A visit to the hot springs resort of Gross Barmen, 26 km to the southwest, is a worthwhile detour from Okahandja.

Accommodation at Gross Barmen ranges from single rooms to bungalows and campsites. Amenities include a restaurant, shop, glass-enclosed thermal hall, outdoor swimming pool and tennis courts. The resort is popular with day visitors over weekends, but it is quiet in the week except during school holidays.

The final stretch back to Windhoek is a pleasant 69-km drive along the Windhoek Valley.

Top: *Among the 2 500 rock engravings at Twyfelfontein is this easily identifiable lion with its L-shaped tail.*
Above: *The Namaqua chameleon is one of the many small creatures inhabiting the harsh Namib Desert and adjoining Kaokoveld.*
Right: *Gemsbok have become adapted to arid conditions and can tolerate body temperatures of up to 45 degrees Centigrade.*
Following pages: *A seemingly endless road strikes through the dry Kaokoveld landscape with its characteristic clumps of euphorbia bushes.*

The Namib and Southern Namibia

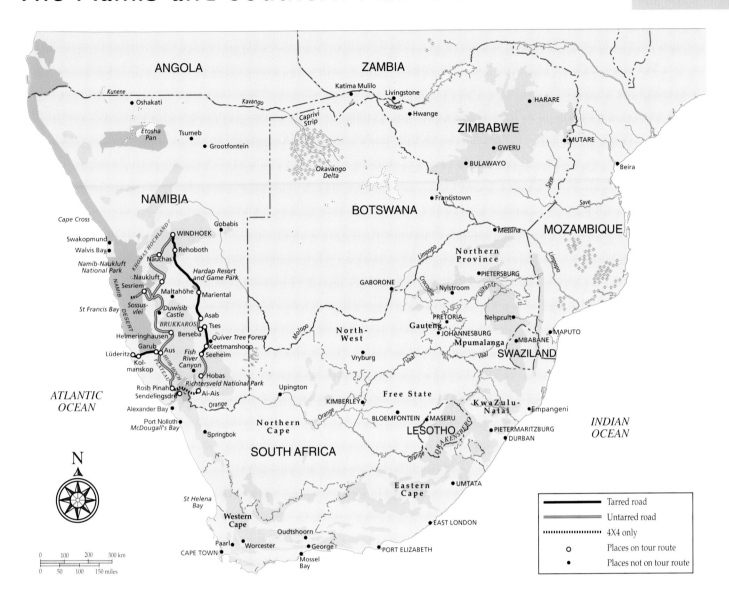

This route combines the spectacular dune landscape of the Namib Desert with the lonely expanses of southern Namibia and the awesome depths of the Fish River Canyon. About a third of the 2 600-km route is on tar, while the remainder is on gravel roads that are generally well maintained. Except for the last 5 km to Sossusvlei, the Naukluft 4x4 Trail and the section between Rosh Pinah and Ai-Ais, this tour can also be done in a sedan car. The tour takes about two weeks to complete.

WINDHOEK
Nestling in the valley created by the Auas Mountain to the south, the Eros Mountains to the east and the Khomas Hochland to the west, Windhoek is a city of striking contrasts. Prominent on the

Opposite: A good way to appreciate the magnificent scenery of Sossusvlei is to scale the humpback dune north of the pan.

skyline to the east is the imposing *Christuskirche* (Church of Christ), the *Tintenpalast*, the seat of the country's parliament, and the *Alte Feste*, an old fort dating back to 1890. In the city's main street, Independence Avenue, impressive German colonial buildings stand alongside modern office blocks. Here executives hurry past Herero ladies dressed in their characteristic Victorian-style dresses, while German beer and *brötchens* are served at pavement cafés. Intersecting Independence Avenue, Post Street Mall bustles with traders selling a variety of African handicrafts.

KHOMAS HOCHLAND AND SPREETSHOOGTE PASS
Leaving Windhoek along Mandume Ndemufayo Road, the route ascends to the Khomas Hochland along the Kupferberg Pass. It then continues across the rolling hills of the Khomas Hochland, with the table-top Gamsberg becoming increasingly prominent

Above: *Rugged mountains and an ancient camel thorn tree form a backdrop to Sesriem campsite, gateway to one of Namibia's most remarkable attractions, Sossusvlei.*

to the southwest. This 2 347-m-high mountain, the third highest in Namibia, owes its distinctive shape to the quartzite capping that protects the underlying granite against erosion.

Further along, take the route to Nauchas farm; turn right here and continue to Spreetshoogte Pass with its dazzling view over the Namib Desert below. With a gradient of 1:4,5 to 1:6, it is the steepest pass in Namibia. From the summit the road descends the escarpment in a series of sweeping curves and hairpin bends.

On joining the Walvis Bay/Maltahöhe road, proceed to the farm Bullsport, where petrol can be obtained. The route now continues to the entrance gate of the Naukluft section of the Namib-Naukluft Park, the office being 11 km further.

NAUKLUFT 4x4 TRAIL

Situated on the eastern edge of the Namib, the Naukluft section of the park is a world of rugged mountain peaks, sheer cliffs and deep valleys with hidden springs. It was proclaimed in 1968 as a sanctuary for the Hartmann's mountain zebra, which occurs only in Namibia and southwestern Angola.

Visitors are lured to Naukluft's small campsite by its tranquil atmosphere and delightful mountain pools. Owing to the ruggedness of the terrain, the area can be explored only by four-wheel drive vehicle or on foot. In addition to two day walks, you can also go on an overnight hiking trail that can be completed in either four or eight days.

Covering 72 km, the Naukluft 4x4 Trail traverses countryside that ranges from narrow, winding mountain passes and steep inclines to rocky river-beds. Off-road driving skills are tested to the limit on this two-day route, but the rewards are great. Several viewpoints offer magnificent vistas of the plains and valleys below and the Zaris Mountains in the distance. Places of interest along the route have been marked and are explained in the trail brochure. Among the game species to be seen are Hartmann's mountain zebra, gemsbok, springbok, klipspringer and baboon.

Tjeriktik campsite, at the end of the first day's journey, is situated in a secluded valley high up in the mountains. It has four A-frame stone huts, a central braai area, a shower and toilet.

From Naukluft, the route follows the valley chiselled between the Naukluft and Zaris mountains by the Tsauchab River, and then heads north to Sesriem.

SESRIEM

This delightful campsite is named after the nearby canyon where the early pioneers used to obtain water by lowering a bucket tied to six ox thongs to the pools in the 30-metre-deep canyon. From the parking area above the canyon, a footpath descends along a gully to the canyon floor, revealing the various layers of conglomerate laid down millions of years ago.

Sesriem campsite, with its enormous camel thorn trees, is the gateway to one of Namibia's most popular tourist attractions, Sossusvlei. Amenities at the campsite include a shop, swimming pool and filling station. The adjacent Sossusvlei Karos Lodge offers luxury accommodation in units that combine the structure of Arab villages with the tented homes of the Bedouins.

From the Sesriem campsite the route heads west along the wide valley of the Tsauchab River. The valley is flanked by high dunes with sinuous crests, seen at their best shortly after sunrise when the dark shaded slopes are in sharp contrast to the slopes catching the first rays of the sun. On the northern side of the valley the dunes soar up to 325 m skywards, placing them among the highest in the world.

About 60 km from Sesriem the gravel road gives way to a sandy track, negotiable only by four-wheel drive vehicle. After 5 km the track ends at Sossusvlei, a white clay pan surrounded by magnificent dunes. Swamped by the encroaching dunes of the Namib Desert tens of thousands of years ago, the pan marks the end of the Tsauchab River's journey to the sea. More often than not the pan is dry, and up to a decade can go by before the flood waters of the Tsauchab reach this far.

DUWISIB CASTLE

The road now traverses the gravel plains below the escarpment in a southeasterly direction, and then follows a valley between the Nubib and Zaris mountains. It ascends the escarpment along the scenic Zarishoogte (Zaris Heights) towards Maltahöhe, continuing along back roads to Duwisib.

Most travellers chance quite unexpectedly upon Duwisib, an imposing stone castle in Neo-Romanesque style. Set amongst rolling hills to the southwest of Maltahöhe, the castle was built in 1908/9 by the illustrious Captain Hans-Heinrich von Wolf. The focal point of the 22-roomed fortress is the main hall or *Rittersaal* which is flanked by sitting rooms. Upstairs is the *Herrenzimmer* (a room reserved for men) and a minstrels' gallery immediately above the imposing front door.

Except for the stone, which was quarried nearby, all the material and the furniture were imported from Europe and transported by ox-wagon from Lüderitz. Adorning the walls are swords, rifles, etchings and paintings of Von Wolf, and some of the castle's original furniture is displayed.

Von Wolf, a German military officer, had a passion for horses, and imported and bred fine specimens. It has been suggested that the wild horses of the Namib are descendants of his stud.

Near the entrance gate is a campsite with hot water ablutions, tables and benches, as well as fireplaces.

WILD HORSES OF GARUB

From Duwisib you follow a back road to Helmeringhausen, a farming settlement nestling between the Rooirand (Red Ridge) and the Schwartzrand (Black Ridge). Here you will find a hotel, a filling station and an interesting Agricultural Museum. Continuing in a southwesterly direction, the road winds its way through the Rooirand, laced with black dolerite boulders, and then traverses the remarkable Neisip Plains.

Just outside the small settlement of Aus the route joins the tar road to Lüderitz, and a few kilometres beyond Aus you enter the *Sperrgebiet* (Forbidden Territory) of Diamond Area No. 1. The area was proclaimed by the German colonial administration in

1908 to award exclusive prospecting and diamond mining rights to the *Deutsche Kolonialgesellschaft für Südwestafrika*. The rights over the *Sperrgebiet* were subsequently bought by the mining giant Consolidated Diamond Mines, now known as NAMDEB.

As you continue westwards to Lüderitz, the plains to the northwest are interrupted by an isolated outcrop, Dikwillem, which once served as a heliograph station. Keep an eye out for the wild horses of the Namib which are usually seen near Garub, where water is supplied for them by pumping it into a trough. The average population is usually about 150–160, but in 1992 numbers stood at 267. A severe drought the following year prompted the Ministry of Environment and Tourism to catch 104 horses and put them up for sale. Visitors can enjoy close-up views of these renowned horses from the hide near the water trough.

LÜDERITZ

Grasplatz, a small railway station overlooked by a lonely double-storeyed house, marks the site where the first diamond was discovered in the region in April 1908. Just a few kilometres further, the ghost town of Kolmanskop comes into view. Once the centre of the country's diamond industry, Kolmanskop fell into a state of disrepair when mining operations ceased in 1950.

Below: Accommodation at Sossusvlei Karos Lodge is a blend of Bedouin tents and the adobe-style walls of an Arab village.

Above: *After good rains the usually drab Namib plains are transformed into a colourful floral spectacle.*

Great amounts of sand infiltrated the buildings through windows and doors, roofing material was blown off by the fierce winds, the salt-laden fog gnawed away at the woodwork and in time the once bustling mining town became a ghost of its former self. Guided tours of Kolmanskop are conducted daily.

Lüderitz, with its beautiful old German-style buildings, has largely retained its continental atmosphere and is best explored on foot. Allow at least two full days to discover the charms of this harbour town. Among its architectural treasures are the *Felsenkirche*, the old post office, Kreplin House, Goerke House, the station building and the *Altstadt* area. The small but interesting Lüderitz Museum depicts the early history of the area. Not to be missed is a drive around the Lüderitz Peninsula and a yacht trip in Lüderitz Bay on board the schooner *Sedina*.

GAMKAB RIVER VALLEY
From Lüderitz, backtrack to Aus and then head in a southerly direction to the mining settlement at Rosh Pinah, where zinc is mined. From here a track leads south to Sendelingsdrif on the northern banks of the Orange River and then meanders eastwards along the river through splendid mountain scenery. To the south of the Orange River lies the craggy mountain desert of the Richtersveld, while the northern banks of the river are dominated by outliers of the Namus and Huns mountains. After heavy rains the causeway across the Fish River and sections of the road are washed away, so you should enquire about the state of the roads when travelling along this section in the rainy season.

The Orange River is very popular with canoeists seeking the thrills and spills offered by its grade two rapids, and you will often encounter organized groups on the river.

The barren and seemingly inhospitable landscape belies the wealth of succulent plants restricted to this area. Chief among the floral attractions are the intriguing elephant's trunk or *halfmens*, but many other succulents and aloe species also abound.

At the mouth of the Gamkab River the trail splits off to the left and, after making its way through a narrow gorge, the route then continues along the broad valley of the Gamkab until it joins up with the Ai-Ais road.

AI-AIS HOT SPRINGS RESORT
The focal point of this resort on the banks of the Fish River is the hot spring that surfaces here. Set amongst scenery which is reminiscent of a lunar landscape, the resort has a modern indoor spa and a large outdoor swimming pool, fed by the mineral-rich water of the nearby spring.

Accommodation ranges from luxury flats to simple huts and campsites with power points, communal kitchens and hot and cold water ablutions. The rest camp also has a restaurant and a well-stocked shop. During the summer months temperatures of over 40 degrees Centigrade are the rule rather than the exception and the resort is consequently open only from the second Friday in March to 31 October.

FISH RIVER CANYON
Some 65 km north of Ai-Ais lies the awe-inspiring Fish River Canyon. With a depth of up to 549 m and a width of up to 27 km, it is surpassed in size only by Arizona's Grand Canyon.

Several viewpoints on the eastern rim of the canyon afford visitors magnificent vistas of the grandeur of this natural wonder. It consists of a canyon within a canyon – the upper canyon was formed when the ancient valley subsided, while the lower canyon was incised by the river.

Between May and September groups of up to 40 backpackers set off from the northernmost viewpoint to hike the Fish River Canyon Trail to Ai-Ais. The 85-km trail, one of the toughest in Southern Africa, is a constant battle against loose sand, ankle-twisting boulders and stones. Despite its reputation, it is also one of the most popular routes in Southern Africa.

Hobas, about 10 km from the canyon, caters for the camping fraternity and is open throughout the year. It offers shaded campsites with braai facilities, hot and cold water ablutions, a swimming pool and a kiosk stocked with basic food supplies.

From Hobas, the route continues to Holoog, passing the scenic Naute Dam before reaching Seeheim, where it joins the tar road to Keetmanshoop.

BRUKKAROS

On leaving Keetmanshoop, a detour to the Quiver Tree Forest, with its dense concentration of quiver trees, and the Giant's Playground, a conglomeration of precariously balanced rock, will compensate the traveller with some impressive scenery. The turnoff is signposted a few kilometres north of Keetmanshoop.

Continuing further north, the road traverses the vast, sparsely vegetated plains of the Karas region, suited to hardy breeds such as karakul sheep. Rising 600 m above the surrounding plains, the extinct volcano of Brukkaros becomes increasingly dominant as you approach the Nama settlement of Tses. Turn left at Tses and drive on to the turnoff to Brukkaros. After 11 km the track ends at the base of the volcano, and from here it is an hour's walk into the crater. Once inside the crater, it is quite a steep slog to the crater rim, but the dramatic view provides ample reward.

Brukkaros was formed some 80 million years ago when molten rock intruded into the rocks about a kilometre below the surface. Steam from the underground water caused the overlying rock to form a dome and, as a result, more magma intruded into the dome. Superheated steam from below then blew out the centre of the dome, thereby forming the crater.

You will reach Berseba, a Nama settlement which developed around the mission station established here in 1850, about 1 km beyond the Brukkaros turnoff. From here the route proceeds along a back road and, after crossing the Fish River, goes on to Asab where you will rejoin the tar B1 road.

HARDAP DAM

Heading towards Windhoek, the road bypasses Mariental (the centre of Namibia's ostrich industry) and then reaches the turn-off to the Hardap Resort and Game Park. The resort lies on the banks of the the Hardap Dam (the country's largest dam) and is favoured by watersport enthusiasts. It offers some of the finest freshwater fishing in the country and is a haven for waterbirds, including a large breeding population of white pelicans.

Surrounding the dam is a game park stocked with gemsbok, springbok, red hartebeest, kudu, eland, black rhino and ostrich. The park also has a 15-km circular trail, with a shorter 9-km loop, for those wanting to explore the area on foot.

Accommodation at Hardap ranges from bungalows to campsites. Other amenities include a restaurant with a superb view over the dam, a shop, swimming pool and filling station.

The last 260 km back to Windhoek is an easy drive through Rehoboth with its hot spring resort and the nearby Oanob Dam. The Rehoboth Museum has exhibits depicting local history and archaeological finds, natural history and traditional houses.

Below: Viewpoints along the eastern rim of the Fish River Canyon provide awe-inspiring vistas.

Left: *At sunrise the deep orange glow of the dunes at Sossusvlei contrasts sharply with the dark shadows on the slopes.*
Top: *The Quiver Tree Forest near Keetmanshoop contains an unusually dense concentration of about 250 quiver trees.*
Above: *Streaks of light create abstract patterns in an abandoned building in the ghost village of Kolmanskop, just outside Lüderitz.*
Following pages: *The* Felsenkirche, *or Church on the Rocks, towers above Lüderitz and is a familiar landmark.*

Bushmanland and Etosha

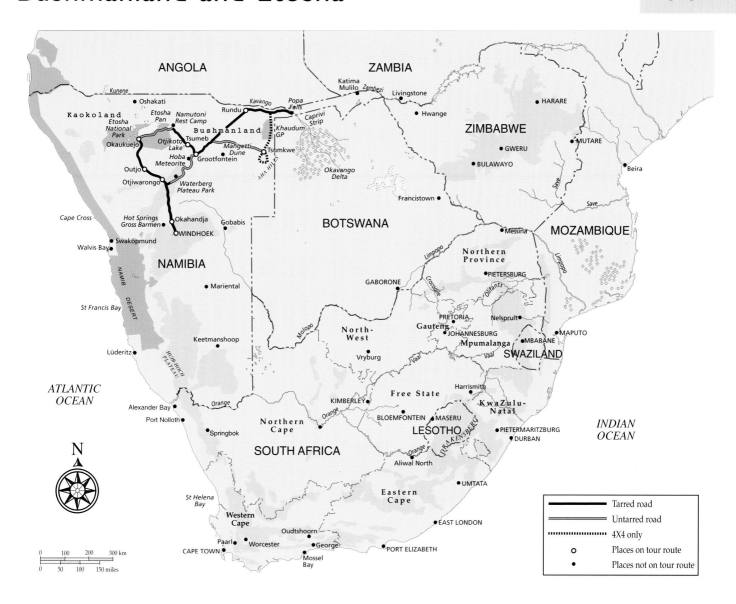

The remote eastern part of Namibia is a vast expanse of Kalahari sand, woodlands and the ancestral home of one of Southern Africa's last few groups of San people. Khaudum Game Park, to the north of Bushmanland, is the heartland of Namibia's roan population, large herds of elephant, the endangered wild dog and a variety of other species. However, the attraction of this game park is not so much its wildlife, but its solitude, isolation and wilderness atmosphere. This tour also includes the flagship of Namibia's conservation areas, the Etosha National Park.

Owing to the sandy terrain and remoteness of Bushmanland and Khaudum Game Park, a four-wheel drive vehicle is essential for this 2 900-km tour, and groups should consist of at least two four-wheel drive vehicles. Allow a minimum of two weeks.

Opposite: *The roots of this hardy rock fig are anchored in the red sandstone of the Waterberg Plateau Park.*

From Windhoek, follow the B1 north to Okahandja, a small town known as the garden town of Namibia. The Okahandja *Backerei,* with its mouth-watering breakfast menu and German confectionary, is an ideal breakfast or tea stop. From Okahandja, continue north along the B1 until you reach the signposted turn-off to the Waterberg Plateau Park, south of Otjiwarongo.

WATERBERG PLATEAU PARK

Rising above the surrounding thornveld of the Otjozondjupa region, the Waterberg is a sandstone relic of a highland which once covered a lage section of the northern part of Namibia. The mountain is named after the abundance of water seeping from the springs on its lower slopes, where enormous sycamore figs, buffalo thorns, weeping wattles and ferns flourish.

The rest camp in the Waterberg Plateau Park has quite a number of short walks, and during an early morning or late

161

Above: Several enormous baobab trees tower above the wood-lands and tree savanna of Eastern Bushmanland in Namibia.

afternoon walk it is not unusual to see the dainty dik-dik, a family of banded mongooses or even a bushbaby. A short walk to watch the sunset from Mountain View on the plateau is a beautiful experience, but remember to allow yourself enough time to return to the rest camp before dark. The face-brick chalets of the modern rest camp blend in exceptionally well with their surroundings; campsites are also available. Other amenities include a restaurant in the historic *Rasthaus* – which served as a police station between 1910 and 1955 – a swimming pool, shop and filling station.

The plateau is home to a variety of game, including white and black rhino, buffalo, giraffe, eland, gemsbok, impala, kudu and roan. Birdlife is prolific and includes Namibia's only breeding colony of the Cape vulture. Private vehicles are not allowed onto the plateau, but guided game-viewing drives are conducted daily.

The more energetic visitor can explore the plateau on foot, either by undertaking a guided wilderness trail or by embarking upon the four-day self-guided hiking trail.

From Waterberg Plateau Park the route continues along back roads through one of the country's prime cattle-farming areas.

HOBA METEORITE

On joining the B8, take the signposted turnoff (D2860) to the Hoba Meteorite near Grootfontein. Measuring nearly 3 m in length and width, and with a mass of 60 tonnes, this is the largest meteorite in the world and has a unique cuboid shape.

The Hoba meteorite belongs to the group of iron meteorites, consisting mainly of iron (82,6 per cent), nickel (16,4 per cent) and cobalt (0,76 per cent), with additional minute traces of carbon, sulphur, chromium, zinc, copper and gallium.

It has been suggested that the meteorite struck the earth some 80 thousand years ago. Although it appears to have formed a small crater, there is no evidence that the crater was formed by the meteorite. After colliding with the earth, the meteorite was gradually covered by calcrete and when it was first described in 1920 only a small part of it was protruding above the ground.

GROOTFONTEIN

The town of Grootfontein is an important centre serving the surrounding maize- and cattle-farming communities. The town developed around a fountain, hence its name, and is characterized by an abundance of trees. Take the time to visit the Grootfontein Museum, housed in the *Alte Feste*, a historic fort dating back to 1896. Displays depict the history of the town and the surrounding areas, and the museum also houses excellent reconstructions of both a carpenter's shop and a blacksmith's workshop. Also of interest is a mineral collection and displays on traditional craft.

From Grootfontein, follow the B8 towards Rundu for 55 km and then turn onto the Tsumkwe road, continuing eastwards for 72 km on the C44. The availability of fuel in Tsumkwe is quite unreliable and you are therefore advised to fill up at the farm Hieromtrent. The turnoff to the farm, 12 km south of the C44, is clearly signposted shortly before you reach the veterinary fence. You should take on enough fuel for a journey of at least 600 km to the next refuelling stop at Divundu, bearing in mind that the sandy tracks of the Khaudum Game Park (*see* page 164) require frequent use of four-wheel drive low range. The veterinary fence is reached 3 km east of the turnoff to Hieromtrent. Also known as the Red Line, the fence demarcates the western boundary of the area known as Bushmanland.

BUSHMANLAND

From the Red Line the road continues in an easterly direction, passing through the magnificent Kalahari woodlands of western Bushmanland. San (Bushman) settlements are found at Mangetti Dune and Luhebu, but the inhabitants are not indigenous to the area. They are in fact displaced Vasekela who fled to the Caprivi Strip after the civil war broke out in Angola in 1976. Some of them subsequently joined the South African Defence Force and were resettled at the military base at Mangetti Dune.

Continuing eastwards, you will reach Eastern Bushmanland about 40 km beyond Mangetti. This region is the ancestral land of approximately 2 000 Ju/'hoan San people, who live in scattered communities throughout the 890 000-ha area. Like the San elsewhere in Southern Africa, the Ju/'hoan have also been affected by numerous changes and, contrary to postcard images, they no longer walk around in loincloths with a bow and arrow slung over their shoulders. They live in several small settlements throughout the area, practising a subsistence economy of dryland crop production and cattle farming, and supplementing their diet with veld foods.

The area east of Tsumkwe is characterized by a cluster of small vegetated pans, known as the Pannetjiesveld, while the two Dobe pans lie further to the north. South of Tsumkwe are Nyae-Nyae and Khebi, two large calcrete pans. During the late winter the pans are dry, but after good summer rains they flood onto the woodlands, inundating an area of up to 120 000 square kilometres. A variety of waterbirds are attracted to the pans and in excess of 11 000 birds, including thousands of flamingoes, have been counted on Nyae-Nyae Pan.

Dotted about the landscape are clusters of baobab trees that have long served as landmarks for travellers. Two particularly well-known trees southeast of Tsumkwe are the Holboom near Tsokwe and the Grootboom at Homasi. The Holboom is named after a large cavity in the centre of its trunk, while the gigantic Grootboom has a circumference of over 30 m.

Since the southern boundary of the Khaudum Game Park is unfenced, game numbers fluctuate seasonally. Species include elephant, gemsbok, kudu, blue wildebeest, red hartebeest, roan, buffalo and tsessebe. In addition to wild dog, small numbers of lion, cheetah, leopard and both species of hyena also occur.

Situated in the far eastern region of Bushmanland and rising about 70 m above the surrounding landscape, the Aha Hills are a 40-km-long range of marble, dolomite and limestone extending into Botswana. The only eminence in a vast area, the hills offer far-reaching views across Bushmanland and Botswana.

The very sandy terrain of Bushmanland and the adjacent Khaudum Game Park necessitates the use of a four-wheel drive vehicle. Groups should consist of at least two vehicles and after

Below: The Ju/'hoan San people of Eastern Bushmanland have become caught up between pursuing their traditional way of life and adapting to Western influences.

summer rains regular stops should be made to inspect whether grass has been caught up in the protection plate. In summer, caution should be exercised in areas with clayish soil as there is a good chance of getting bogged down.

From Tsumkwe, the route follows a sandy track northwards to the Khaudum Game Park. About 34 km beyond Tsumkwe, a turnoff to the right leads to another well-known baobab, the Dorslandboom. The name of the tree is a reminder of the Dorsland Trekkers who camped here in the 1880s during their epic journey from the then Transvaal to Angola.

KHAUDUM GAME PARK

This park covers 384 000 ha of Kalahari sandveld and shares its eastern boundary with the Namibia/Botswana border. It is a stronghold of one of Southern Africa's endangered antelope species, the roan. Large numbers of elephant occur in winter, but after the summer rains they disperse widely and leave the park. Other frequent sightings include giraffe, blue wildebeest, gemsbok, kudu and steenbok. Less commonly seen are eland, tsessebe, red hartebeest and reedbuck.

Although the dry winter months are the most rewarding for game viewing, the summer rains bring the migrant birds, and excellent birding opportunities. Among the migrant birds are white and Abdim's storks, yellowbilled kite, steppe and lesser spotted eagles, Western redfooted kestrel, ruff, European, blue-cheeked and carmine bee-eaters, redbreasted swallow and the African golden oriole. Since the tracks are sandy, driving is much easier during the summer months, but crossing the *omiramba* (seasonally inundated fossil rivers) can present problems.

Amenities in the park are limited to two small rest camps: Sikereti in the south and Khaudum in the north. Rustic reed-and-thatch huts are available at both rest camps, as well as basic campsites. Unlike the other rest camps in Namibia, these are unfenced and visitors should bear in mind that potentially dangerous animals could pass through the camps.

The track from Khaudum Camp to Katere on the B8 linking Rundu and Katima Mulilo consists of deep, loose sand, requiring constant use of low range. On reaching the tar road, turn east and head for Divundu. Look for the signposted turnoff to Popa Falls Rest Camp, which you reach after 5 km on a gravel road.

POPA FALLS

After a few days in the sandveld wilderness of Khaudum, Popa Falls on the Kavango River is a most welcome sight. The distant roar of the rapids, the shady riverine trees and the ever-present song of birds all create a very peaceful atmosphere. Popa is an ideal base for exploring the nearby Mahango Game Park.

At Popa Falls you can either link up with Tour 8 (*see* page 99) or continue westwards to include Etosha in your tour.

RUNDU

From Divundu, the tar road strikes westwards for 200 km to Rundu, capital of the Kavango region. Far more scenic, though, is the old gravel road which follows the course of the Kavango River, the lifeblood of the Kavango's inhabitants. Nearly 80 per cent of the population live close to the river. Fish is an important part of the diet of the Kavango people, while reeds are used for the weaving of mats. Maize, *omahangu* (millet) and sorghum are cultivated on the fertile banks of the river.

The Kavango people are skilled woodcarvers and their household articles (such as bowls and dishes), as well as items of furniture with very attractive designs, are crafted from teak, locally known as *dolfhout*. Be sure to pay a visit to the Mbangura Woodcarvers' Cooperative shop in Rundu, where you can buy the works of these woodcarvers.

Accommodation in and around Rundu ranges from guest houses and bungalows to lodges, some with campsites.

Below: *Lionesses charging impala at the Okaukuejo waterhole in Etosha National Park.*

TSUMEB

From Rundu, the route continues on tar to Grootfontein and then to Tsumeb, a pleasant mining town. During its 90-year lifespan, the Tsumeb copper mine became world famous for its minerals, among them aragonite, malachite, dioptase and cerussite. Some of these can be seen in the Tsumeb Museum in Main Street, which also boasts a fascinating display of the German armaments recovered from Otjikoto Lake.

From Tsumeb take the Oshakati/Ondangwa road, stopping at Otjikoto Lake, an enormous sinkhole formed when the roof of an underground cavern in the dolomite rock collapsed. The lake is about 55 m deep and measures 100 m by 150 m in diameter. Large quantities of ammunition and armaments were dumped into the lake in 1915 by the German forces retreating ahead of the South African forces that had invaded the country.

Schools of the small, brightly-coloured Otjikoto tilapia, an endangered species occurring only in Otjikoto and nearby Guinas, can be seen swimming near the lake's surface. The colours of the fish range from greyish-green to black, while some are bright yellow with black stripes, and variegated blue, white and black.

If you continue on the Oshakati/Ondangwa road, the turnoff to Guinas Lake is clearly signposted. A detour to the lake, set amidst very attractive surroundings, is well worth the effort.

The turnoff to Etosha National Park is 82 km beyond Tsumeb and from here it is a further 24 km to the eastern gate.

ETOSHA NATIONAL PARK

One of Africa's great game parks, Etosha National Park is centred around the vast Etosha Pan. It is Namibia's most popular tourist destination, its main attraction being the relative ease with which game can be seen especially during the dry winter months. Herds

Above: Namutoni Rest Camp in the east of Etosha National Park offers accommodation in the historic fort.

of gemsbok, springbok and blue wildebeest grace the grasslands on the edge of the Etosha Pan, while the woodlands support red hartebeest and kudu. In winter, large numbers of elephant concentrate around the waterholes, but during the rainy season they disperse widely throughout the park.

Etosha has one of the world's largest populations of the endangered black rhino and a small population of white rhinos, reintroduced here in 1995. It is also the habitat of the black-faced impala, a species restricted to northwestern Namibia and southwestern Angola, and is one of the best places to see the Damara dik-dik. The park is renowned for its lions, while leopard, cheetah and spotted hyena also occur.

Etosha's three rest camps, Namutoni, Halali and Okaukuejo, offer accommodation ranging from rooms in the gracious Fort Namutoni and modern chalets to camping sites. Amenities at each of the rest camps include a swimming pool, a restaurant and a shop where groceries, frozen meat, liquor and curios can be bought. Although the waterhole situated on the perimeter of Okaukuejo is the best known, Namutoni and Halali also have waterholes. Luxury accommodation is available at Mokuti Lodge, which borders on the park at Von Lindequist Gate near Namutoni, and at Ongava Lodge near Andersson Gate, south of Okaukuejo Rest Camp.

The 435-km journey from Okaukuejo to Windhoek is all on tar and is easily completed in about five hours. The route passes through Outjo and Otjiwarongo, where the Crocodile Ranch is well worth a visit. Travel south from Otjiwarongo, returning to Windhoek along the same road used at the start of the tour.

Left: *Etosha is home to about 1 500 elephants. During the dry winter months they congregate around the waterholes, but after the summer rains they disperse widely throughout the park.*
Above: *In the heat of summer the swimming pool at Etosha's Okaukeujo Rest Camp is much appreciated.*
Following pages: *Giraffe, Burchell's zebra and eland quenching their thirst at one of the many waterholes in Etosha National Park.*

Useful addresses and telephone numbers

AUTOMOBILE ASSOCIATIONS

NAMIBIA
Automobile Association of Namibia
P O Box 61
Windhoek
Tel: (+26461) 22-4201; fax: 22-2446

SOUTH AFRICA
Automobile Association of South Africa
P O Box 596
Johannesburg 2000
Tel: (011) 799-1000; fax: 466-2572

ZIMBABWE
Automobile Association of Zimbabwe
P O Box 585
Harare
Tel: (+2634) 75-2779; fax: 75-2522

CONSERVATION AUTHORITIES

BOTSWANA
Director of Wildlife and National Parks
P O Box 131
Gaborone
Tel: (+267) 37-1405; fax: 31-2354
(Central Kalahari Game Reserve, Gemsbok National Park [including Mabuasehube] and Khutse Game Reserve)

Director of Wildlife and National Parks
P O Box 20364
Boseja
Maun
Tel: (+267) 66-1265; fax: 66-1264
(Chobe National Park, Makgadikgadi Pans National Park, Moremi Game Reserve and Nxai Pan National Park)

Opposite: The barren landscape near the Quiver Tree Forest, Keetmanshoop, is brightened by this colourful scarecrow.

LESOTHO
Lesotho National Park, Ministry of Agriculture
P O Box 92
Maseru, 100
Tel: (+266) 32-3600; fax: 31-0349
(Sehlabathebe National Park)

MOZAMBIQUE
The Director
Direção Nacional de Flora e Fauna
Bravia
Ministerio da Agricultura
Praça dos Herois
Maputo
Tel: (+2581) 46-0548; fax: 46-0547
(Bazaruto and Gorongosa national parks, Maputo Elephant Reserve)

NAMIBIA
Director of Tourism
Reservations
Private Bag 13267
Windhoek
Tel: (+26461) 23-6975;
fax: 22-4900
(Ai-Ais Hot Springs and Fish River Canyon, Caprivi and Daan Viljoen game parks, Etosha National Park, Gross Barmen Hot Springs Resort, Hardap Resort and Game Park, Khaudum and Mahango game parks, Mamili and Mudumu national parks, Namib-Naukluft Park, Popa Falls Game Park, Reho Spa and Von Bach recreation resorts and Waterberg Plateau Park)

SOUTH AFRICA
Cape Nature Conservation
Citrusdal District Office
Private Bag X1
Citrusdal 7340
Tel: (022) 921-2289;
fax: 921-3219

National Parks Board of South Africa
P O Box 787
Pretoria 0001

General Enquiries – tel: (012) 343-9770; fax: 343-9958
Reservations – tel: (012) 343-1991; fax: 343-0905

National Parks Board of South Africa
P O Box 7400
Roggebaai 8012
General Enquiries – tel: (021) 22-2816; fax: 24-6211
Reservations – tel: (021) 22-2810; fax: 24-6211
(Augrabies Falls, Golden Gate Highlands, Kalahari Gemsbok, Karoo, Kruger, Marakele and Richtersveld national parks)

Natal Parks Board
P O Box 1750
Pietermaritzburg 3200
General enquiries – tel: (0331) 47-1961; fax: 47-1037
Reservations – tel: (0331) 47-1981; fax: 47-1980
(Hluhluwe-Umfolozi Park, Greater St Lucia Wetland Park, [including Mkuzi Game Reserve], Natal Drakensberg Park)

Department of Nature Conservation KwaZulu-Natal
Private Bag X9024
Pietermaritzburg 3200
Tel: (0331) 47-3272; fax: 47-3795
(Kosi Bay Coastal Forest Reserve [including Kosi Bay Nature Reserve and Lake Sibaya], Ndumo Game Reserve and Tembe Elephant Park)

The Reserve Manager
Goegap Nature Reserve
Private Bag X1
Springbok 8240
Tel: (0251) 2-1880; fax: 8-1286

The Reserve Manager
Witsand Nature Reserve
Private Bag X3006
Postmasburg 8420
Tel: (0591) 7-2373

QwaQwa Highlands National Park
P O Box 403
Kestell 9860
Tel: (058) 713-1608; fax: 713-5302

SWAZILAND
Mlilwane Wildlife Sanctuary
Central Reservations
P O Box 234
Mbabane
Tel: (+268) 4-5006; fax: 6-1594

Malolotja Nature Reserve
Central Reservations
P O Box 100
Mbabane
Tel: (+264) 6-1178; fax: 6-1875

ZAMBIA
The Chief Warden
National Parks and Wildlife Service
Private Bag 1
Chilanga
Tel: (+2601) 27-8187
(Sioma Ngwezi and Kafue
national parks)

ZIMBABWE
The Director
National Parks and Wildlife
Management
P O Box CY 826
Causeway
Harare
Tel: (+2634) 70-6077; fax: 72-6089
(Bunga Forest Botanical Reserve,
Bvumba Botanical Gardens, Lake
Mutirikwi Recreational Park,
Chimanimani, Chizarira, Ewanrigg,
Gonarezhou, Great Zimbabwe,
Hwange, Mana Pools, Matusadona,
Nyanga, Victoria Falls and Zambezi
national parks)

MAPS

BOTSWANA
The Director
Department of Lands and Surveys
Private Bag 0037
Gaborone
Tel: (+267) 35-3251; fax: 35-2704

LESOTHO
The Director
Land Survey and Physical Planning
P O Box 876
Maseru, 100
Tel: (+266) 32-2376; fax: 31-1340

MOZAMBIQUE
The Director
DINAGECA (Maps and Land
Attribution)
P O Box 288
Maputo
Tel: (+2581) 30-2555;
fax: 42-1802

NAMIBIA
The Director
Office of the Surveyor-General
Private Bag 13182
Windhoek
Tel: (+26461) 24-5056;
fax: 22-7312

SOUTH AFRICA
**The Chief Director Surveys and
Mapping**
Private Bag X10
Mowbray 7705
Tel: (021) 685-4070; fax: 689-1351

SWAZILAND
Department of Public Works
Surveyor-General Office
P O Box 58
Mbabane
Tel: (+268) 4-2321;
fax: 4-2364

ZAMBIA
Ministry of Lands
Survey Department
P O Box 50397
Lusaka
Tel: (+2601) 25-2288;
fax: 25-0120

ZIMBABWE
Surveyor-General
Private Bag 7701
Causeway
Harare
Tel: (+2634) 70-6081; fax: 73-4646

MEDICAL RESCUE

NAMIBIA
Medrescue Namibia
P O Box 31220
Windhoek
Tel: (+26461) 23-0505; fax: 24-8114

SOUTH AFRICA
Medrescue
P O Box 31880
Braamfontein 2017
Tel: (011) 403-7080; fax: 339-3153

ZAMBIA
Specialty Emergency Services
P O Box 31500
Lusaka
Tel: (+2601) 27-3302; fax: 27-3181

ZIMBABWE
Medical Air Rescue Service
P O Box HG 969
Highlands
Harare
Tel: (+2634) 73-9642; fax: 73-4517

TOURISM BODIES

LESOTHO
Lesotho Tourist Office
P O Box 1378
Maseru
Tel: (+266) 31-2896; fax: 31-0108

NAMIBIA
Namibia Tourism
Private Bag 13346
Windhoek
Tel: (+26461) 284-2366; fax: 284-2364

SOUTH AFRICA
Satour
Private Bag X164
Pretoria 0001
Tel: (012) 347-0600; fax: 45-4889

ZAMBIA
Zambia National Tourist Board
P O Box 591232
Kengray 2100
South Africa

Tel: (011) 622-7635;
fax: 622-7424

ZIMBABWE
Zimbabwe Tourism Authority
P O Box 9398
Johannesburg 2000
South Africa
Tel: (011) 331-3137;
fax: 331-6175

FOUR-BY-FOUR TRAILS & COURSES

NAMIBIA
Naukluft 4x4 Trail
See Conservation Authorities:
Director of Tourism,
Namibia

SOUTH AFRICA
Hexvallei 4x4 Trail
Enquiries – tel: (02322) 2114

Kalahari 4x4 Trail
Joppie Botes
Tel: (054) 2-4971;
cell: 083 305-4227

Karoo 4x4 Trail
Karoo National Park
P O Box 316
Beaufort West 6970
Tel: (0201) 5-2828; fax: 5-1671

Namaqualand 4x4 Trail
Namaqualand District Council
P O Box 5
Springbok 8240
Tel: (0251) 2-2011; fax: 2-1421

Osseberg 4x4 Trail
The Reserve Manager
Baviaanskloof Wilderness Area
P O Box 218
Patensie 6335
Tel: (042) 283-0270;
fax: 283-0915

Qwa-Qwa 4x4 Trail
See Conservation Authorities:
QwaQwa Highlands National Park

Richtersveld National Park
P O Box 406
Alexander Bay 8290
Tel: (0256) 831-1506;
fax: 831-1175

Zebra Crossing 4x4 Trail
Gamka Mountain Nature Reserve
Private Bag X21
Oudtshoorn 6620
Tel: (04437) 3-3367

OFF-ROAD TRACKS & COURSES

SOUTH AFRICA
Continental Off-road Academy
P O Box 4515
Rivonia 2128
Tel: (011) 466-1705; fax: 466-1703

Hennops Off-road Trail
P O Box 615
Pretoria 0001
Tel: (012) 371-9360; fax: 371-9360

The Off-road Experience
P O Box 408
Nelspruit 1200
Tel: (013) 753-2551; fax: 753-3578

Below: *The Chitove camping site is situated on the lower Runde River in the Gonarezhou National Park, Zimbabwe.*

Index

Bold type indicates a main entry, ***bold italic*** type indicates a map reference, and *italic* type indicates a picture reference.

GR = Game Reserve; NP = National Park;
NR = Nature Reserve